CATHOLIC PERSPECTIVES

Charismatics

by
James Hitchcock
and
Gloriana Bednarski, RSM

THE THOMAS MORE PRESS
Chicago, Illinois

ISBN 0-88347-114-0

CATHOLIC
PERSPECTIVES

Charismatics

PART ONE

by
James Hitchcock

THE charismatic movement has possibly been the most amazing development of the entire post-conciliar Catholic Church. For one thing, it was totally unforeseen. Of all the voices concerned with the renewal of the Church, some warning of the dangers of change, others predicting entirely happy results, no one predicted anything like the charismatic phenomenon.

It is amazing not only in terms of the form it has taken, a form previously unfamiliar to Catholics, but also in its enormous numerical success. No one knows for certain how many practicing Catholic charismatics there are in the United States, but they probably number in the hundreds of thousands. Furthermore, this growth has been amazingly swift, and it has occurred at a time when almost all other indices of religious practice in America have been declining. The movement has spread to Latin America, Europe, and (possibly to a lesser extent) to Africa, Asia, and Australia.

Obviously a phenomenon of this kind cannot be ignored, and those who dismiss it as ephemeral or as merely silly are whistling in the dark. For good or ill, it is a movement of major importance. Not only is its impact being felt all over the American Church, it is likely to continue to be felt for decades to come, whatever happens to the core movement itself.

What Is Right with the Charismatics?

IT is difficult to believe that a movement which attracts so many enthusiastic and obviously good people could be wholly bad, or that its appeal could be based primarily on evil influences. There must be at least a core of solid religious reality involved, as even most of the charismatics' critics admit.

A few of the more common objections to the movement can be disposed of rather quickly.

Charismatics are overly emotional.

This is largely a matter of personal taste and temperament. There is abundant warrant in historic Christianity for expecting faith to express itself demonstratively and emotionally, although it need not. For a variety of reasons, Catholicism has manifested a rather subdued spirit in modern times. It has not been devoid of feeling, but feelings have not been extravagantly expressed and have often been kept hidden. A highly emotional piety may seem forced or inappropriate, but there is nothing necessarily wrong with it.

The movement is factionalized.

To some extent this seems to be true. Some original leaders of the movement, especially at the University of Notre Dame, have broken with the present leadership and have publicly criticized the later charismatic phenomenon.[1] Even a casual perusal of the very extensive literature of the movement reveals internal conflicts and disagreements, some of which are expressed only obliquely and guardedly.

It is impossible for an outsider to assess any particular division. However, the fact of such conflict, and of such division, is hardly surprising, even while it may be regrettable. The history of the Church shows this happening over and over again, and the presence or absence of internal divisions is not a reliable way of determining the depth or authenticity of any religious movement. Such conflicts are likely to occur whenever people have deep and passionate convictions; thus religious movements are especially prone to splitting.

The movement is Protestant.

This is a charge which for the time being should perhaps be held in abeyance. It is true that the movement has come into being and has formed itself in accord with certain essentially Protestant models and, furthermore, rather late models at that—not classical Protestantism but developments in twentieth-century America.

It is also true that there has been a high degree of inter-denominational activity and cooperation—prayer groups, rallies, magazines, etc. While there is an identifiable Catholic pentecostalism, the boundaries between it and the various Protestant kinds are not sharply drawn.

The uncertainty is in what should be made of

these facts. The Second Vatican Council firmly committed the Catholic Church to ecumenical activity, and it is ironic that the most vigorous such activity should be taking place amidst the sometimes despised charismatics, instead of as a result of the largely sterile and anemic official attempts to ecumenical cooperation.

A related charge is that the movement is outside the confines of the institutional Church, existing almost as a parallel ecclesial structure. There seems to be some truth to this criticism, which will be dealt with later. However, on the whole it seems clear that the national leadership of the movement has made a serious attempt to keep it firmly Catholic, an effort which has not been successful in all cases.

One study has found that Catholic charismatics tend to be more orthodox on most questions than do their non-charismatic peers, except on the question of Christ's having given leadership in the Church to Peter and the popes, where they are somewhat less so.[2] If accurate, this finding does suggest that some Catholic charismatics trim their doctrinal sails to accommodate ecumenical winds.

The most elaborate and widely publicized study of charismatic beliefs and behavior, by a Jesuit sociologist, charges that Catholic charismatics are "heterodox" in three respects: their belief in the imminent Second Coming of Christ, their certitude about their own personal salvation, and their belief that "the Holy Spirit speaks to the heart, not the mind."[3]

In many ways this study seems unfair to the charismatics. For one thing, they were singled out for special scrutiny as to their orthodoxy at a time when such investigations have been loudly declared invalid and even un-Christian. (One can imagine the cries of outrage if a similar investigation were made of Catholics involved in, say, the movement for women's ordination.) Secondly, the criteria of heterodoxy seem eccentric. Catholics are not forbidden to believe in the imminent Second Coming, so long as they do not attempt to make it a dogma of faith. Probably many Catholics who are not charismatics would agree with the statements that "the Holy Spirit speaks to the heart, not the mind" and "accepting Jesus as my personal savior means that I am already saved." A good deal of exegesis of both statements would have to be made before it could be stated with certitude that they imply heterodox beliefs.

The study also puts little emphasis on much more fundamental criteria of orthodoxy which it seems possible that charismatics would accept even more readily than many non-charismatics—the divinity of Christ, the virgin birth, the divine inspiration of the Scriptures, Christ's bodily resurrection.

The fact that some charismatic priests have given up the priesthood, cited as a stricture against the movement,[4] is also unfair, since there is practically no movement in the contemporary Church about which the same could not be said. (If the criterion of priests leaving the priesthood were applied to the social-justice movement, for example, the movement would long ago have been totally discredited.)

Charismatics are fundamentalists.

This is another version of the criticism that they are really Protestants, and the validity of the charge depends mainly on how "fundamentalism" is defined. If it is taken to mean a rigid approach to Scripture, in which the Bible alone is accepted as having authentic teaching authority, and in which the Bible is thought to provide a detailed guide for all aspects of living, then there are fundamentalist tendencies among some Catholic charismatics, although the national leadership of the movement has attempted to keep alive a sense of the teaching authority of the whole Church.

There is another sense in which the term "fundamentalist" is merely a smear word, used by theological liberals to dismiss anyone who believes in the authoritative truth of Scripture, a belief which is basic to Catholicism as well as to classical Protestantism. In this view, anyone who believes that the miracles related in the New Testament really occurred, for example, would be a fundamentalist, as would anyone who thinks that Scripture provides unchanging norms for human behavior.

Charismatics are escapists.

By this is meant that instead of working out their salvation in the midst of the world, charismatics think they have found a direct pipeline to God. Along with this criticism often goes the charge that they have a "negative" view of the world, a stance of criticism and condemnation.

There is a sense in which some charismatics do seem to believe in what Martin Luther called "cheap grace," that is, a sense of consolation and acceptance by God unaccompanied by any necessity of bearing the cross. However, in general it cannot be said that charismatics have found an easier road to salvation than has the average non-charismatic Catholic. Being a genuine charismatic requires a considerable investment of time and energy— weekly prayer meetings (sometimes more than weekly), daily prayers and Bible-readings at home, and, not uncommonly, daily Mass. In addition, being a charismatic demands an intensity about one's spiritual life which most Catholics do not possess. Although the terminology may not be used, the charismatic discipline involves what amounts to frequent examinations of conscience and resolves to amend one's life. A charismatic is expected to live a spiritually strenuous life, taking nothing for granted and striving constantly for improvement.

As to their alleged neglect of the world, most charismatics continue to function in secular occupations, and there is certainly no evidence that they perform their tasks less conscientiously than other people. In all probability their religious commitments make them more conscientious. Where active

11

charismatics neglect the world is probably by spending less time watching television or in amusements generally, which is hardly a criticism of them.

Charismatics are not socially conscious.

Such a charge is difficult either to prove or disprove, since it would require developing criteria of what constitutes social consciousness, then doing an elaborate survey to determine how many charismatics meet those criteria.

One such study has been attempted, by the same Jesuit sociologist who detected signs of heterodoxy among Catholic charismatics. On this point also his analysis seems unfair.

In general he found that Catholic charismatics, especially the better-educated ones, hold liberal opinions on social questions but tend to be activists. But his principal criterion for determining authentic Catholic social consciousness seems almost bizarre —it is support for the Equal Rights Amendment to the United States Constitution, an issue about which many Catholics, quite legitimately, have serious misgivings and on which there is certainly no official Catholic position. However, in his critique of the charismatics, feminist ideology is cited as though its truth were self-evident, and by some strange twist of logic support for women's ordination is taken to be a sign of orthodoxy.[5]

Some charismatics do seem to think that prayer alone is the answer to all social problems, which is a false conception. However, there is no good reason to think that charismatics are less sensitive to the needs of their neighbors than are non-charismatics. It can be argued that their emphasis on personal charity and conversion of heart has a stronger Christian tradition behind it than does the advocacy of social change which is now more fashionable. Not every Christian is required to get involved with causes.

The movement is anti-intellectual.

This is no doubt true of some of its members, as it is true of some members of almost all religious movements. Anti-intellectual Catholics make up a certain stratum of the Church both inside and outside the charismatic movement.

The movement has also, however, attracted some able theologians, who have articulated a sophisticated conception of what it can and should be. These include Fathers Edward O'Connor, Kilian McDonnell, George Montague, Simon Tugwell, and Donald Gelpi.[6] (Several accomplished lay theologians—William Storey, Josephine Massyngberde Ford, and Ralph Keiffer—were once associated but have now broken with the movement.) To be charismatic does not necessarily mean to be ignorant, and the general literature of the movement (such as the magazine *New Covenant*) shows a fair degree of sophistication.

THE criticisms made of the charismatics tend to come from two opposite directions—traditional Catholics who find the movement strange and very Protestant in spirit, and avant-garde Catholics who distrust it because they see it as too religious, or in their words too "fundamentalist." For some people, anyone who claims to have some direct experience of God's power, and who seeks to obey divine commands, is dangerously old-fashioned. (The late Episcopal Bishop James A. Pike, whose later public career largely consisted in being a professional heretic, once pompously warned that pentecostalism constituted "heresy in embryo."[7] A well-known attack on the movement by a former Catholic priest cast its net so wide against religious "enthusiasm" that it ensnared practically everyone except agnostics.)[8]

Perhaps the most important thing that can be said in the charismatics' favor is that they have recognized certain elements which were unquestionably part of New Testament Christianity but which tended to fall into neglect over the centuries—the lively sense of the Spirit's presence, commitment to the lordship of Christ in a very personal way, adoption of a way of life which is simple yet demanding and distinctive. Even certain things which may seem peripheral and which often grate on non-charismatics—emotional outbursts of praise, healing rites, and the vexed matter of speaking in tongues—have clear New Testament warrant. (How far the Church of the New Testament is simply to be replicated in later centuries is another question.)

In a time of widespread religious confusion and loss of fervor, charismatics have a very strong sense of God's existence and of his love for them. They believe fervently that God has revealed his will to human beings, and they sincerely try to obey his will in their lives. Judging the authenticity of anyone's faith is always perilous, but all the external signs indicate that the charismatics' faith is real and active. Anyone with even a superficial acquaintance with the movement knows of people who admit that becoming charismatic saved their faith—they were on the road to doubt and an easy secularism until they encountered the Spirit. Over all, the power and sincerity of the movement cannot help but be impressive.

The movement has also been criticized for its supposed negativity to modern culture. Members often confess to having experienced a sense of confusion and rootlessness before their conversions, and they manifest a "crisis mentality," in which they are required to choose between God and evil. Their acceptance of the Spirit provides them with a source of infallible authority. The growth of the movement is said to follow a pattern: requiring a firm act of commitment from new members, intensive recruiting, perceived opposition and even persecution, and a philosophy of personal change or conversion. It is also said to be in part a reaction against the modernist impulses which are thought to be penetrating the Catholic Church.[9]

Although such attitudes, attributed to the charismatics, are now unfashionable, they obviously have great authority in the Christian tradition, and they seem quite compatible with the spirit of the New Testament Church. Self-consciously modern Christians are likely to react to such attitudes with terms like "rigid," "extremist," "sectarian," and even "paranoid." But the charismatics are right in perceiving that from its beginnings Christianity has always demanded an act of conversion from its adherents, based in part on the necessity of overcoming the influence of a sinful world.

Certain related charismatic beliefs, such as the reality of Satan's influence, speaking in tongues, and healing, have been similarly criticized. All three are things easily misunderstood, abused, and given disproportionate weight by overly credulous people, and not all charismatics have shown the requisite prudence in dealing with them. However, there is no doubt that all three are quite biblical and, whatever emphasis is put on them, have a legitimate place in the Christian Church. In this as in other things, charismatics are people sincerely striving to live up to authentic Christian teaching as they understand it, at a time when many Christians are content to fall into an easy worldliness, continually adjusting their beliefs to fit the newest secular trends.

In summing up what is good about the charismatics, a familiar colloquialism might be used: for many people, the movement has been the only game in town. Because of misconceived applications of the teachings of the Second Vatican Council, familiar Catholic devotions, movements, and organizations have all but collapsed in the past fifteen years, and efforts to provide "updated" substitutes have also largely failed. By the early 1970s most Catholics found themselves in the position of having to settle either for a very routine, low-key, undemanding kind of religion or, if they were looking for something more compelling, to redirect their religious fervor into essentially secular channels.

The charismatic movement appeared at this juncture to present Catholics with the possibility of a fervent, demanding kind of faith which, while unfamiliar in certain ways, seemed to be fundamentally orthodox. The movement made converts with a speed almost unprecedented in modern times. There has also been an unrecognized cultural and social pattern involved here: Prior to the Second Vatican Council, Catholicism seems to have attracted converts, as much as anything, because of its sacred ritual and its intellectualized, carefully systematized doctrines. In the more disordered world since that time, the religious initiative seems to have passed to expressive, informal, directly inspirational kinds of Christianity, something which usually happens in periods of social breakdown. The charismatic movement, which had been

17

in existence since 1900, penetrated the Catholic Church just in time to respond to this cultural shift. For many Catholics it may have had the effect of saving their faith.

What Is Wrong with the Charismatics?

PERHAPS the first question a Catholic will be moved to ask about the charismatic movement is, where was it in all those centuries before about 1966, when the first Catholic charismatic manifestation occurred at Duquesne University in Pittsburgh?

Catholicism places strong emphasis on tradition, on the reality of the historical continuity of the Church from age to age. This does not preclude the emergence of new things in the Church. However, Catholicism always asks how new things are connected to the old things, and in particular Catholicism does not accept the contention that, in its history, the Church can somehow be radically unfaithful to Christ.

The charismatic movement does not overtly make this charge, and perhaps few charismatics consciously believe it. However, the nagging question remains: If the charismatic experience is basic to the Christian life, how is it that so few people have had that experience until the twentieth century? Furthermore, how is it that the charismatic experience entered twentieth-century Christianity through some rather marginal Protestant sects and that its piety seems essentially modeled on those sects? There are important questions about ecclesiology and about divine Providence implied here, questions which the charismatics do not seem prepared to discuss candidly.

As already noted, various kinds of charismatic experiences did occur in the early Church, and hence such experiences cannot be dismissed as foreign to Catholicism. However, despite the fact that over the centuries some Catholic saints may have manifested some charismatic signs (possibly a few instances of speaking in tongues, for example), this kind of piety seems to have been largely dormant for at least 1500 years.

Thus if it is thought to be God's will that his followers be charismatics, the question must be asked how the Church strayed so far from that will for so long. In fact, not only did the "institutional Church" overlook the charismatic reality, almost all the saints and prophets through the ages did also. Although some Catholic spiritual teachers encompassed certain things in their teachings which might be compatible with the charismatic reality, virtually none of them ever sought to recall the Church to this reality in any systematic way. It was a reality which was, seemingly, lost until the 1960s, when it was rediscovered through contact with certain fringe Prottestant sects. In the history of the Church there is not a single saint who can serve as a model of charismatic piety, as that piety is now practiced.

The leaders of the movement insist, no doubt sincerely, that they perceive no conflict between charismatic piety and the institutional Church, and they have been at some pains to insist that Catholic charismatics should be loyal children of the Church. However, it is difficult to avoid the impression that the central question of how the movement relates to the larger Church has been systematically avoided. Verbal assurances of harmony and obedience have been proffered, even as serious tensions seem obvious. There is a sense (which would admittedly be hard to substantiate) that charismatics are prepared to be loyal to the Church so long as they receive at least passive approval from the Church, but that if conflict between the movement and the Church should ever develop, their primary allegiance would be to the movement.

There is a certain anti-institutional strain in charismatic writings. A sympathetic German theologian, for example, explicitly connects the rise of the movement to the decline of ecclesiastical authority.[10] A French theologian almost gullible in his credulity about the movement is also anti-institutional and seems to put himself in the position of defending ancient heresies on the grounds that they were manifestations of the Spirit suppressed by uncomprehending authorities.[11] An American charismatic theologian reads the history of the Church as the story of conflict between prophecy and ritual, with the latter systematically driving the former out of the sanctuary.[12]

Anyone familiar with the history of religion is aware of the fact of recurring tension between its inspirational and its institutional aspects, the first those elements—usually uncontrolled and enthusiastic—which give religion its power and force, the second the way in which it is organized for purposes of long-term survival. All vital religions require both elements, and in their most vital periods they hold both in fruitful balance. As religion becomes tired and merely routine, the institutional elements dominate almost completely, to the point where all forms of inspiration become automatically suspect and the leadership resents any disturbance of its comfortable slumber.

At other periods of history institutions—for reasons often both good and bad—fall into disarray, their authority challenged, their structures ignored or repudiated. At such times there is likely to be a great rush of voices, each claiming to be prophetic, each claiming to embody some new inspiration, each claiming to be the authentic path of renewal which the religion must follow. In each age it is likely that some of these voices will be judged, from the perspective of history and of the religion's own authentic traditions, as really embodying the voice of God. But most will not. Nothing is easier than to become a "prophet" in a time of turmoil and uncertainty, when all things have been called into question and almost any message, if put forth with sufficient flair and emphasis, will attract a following.

The existence of the charismatic movement is based on the contention that there has occured an extraordinary outpouring of prophetic grace in the past dozen years, much of it located in particular segments of the Catholic Church. For the sake of argument, this claim can be allowed, at least as a possibility. It can further be admitted, at least tentatively, that such an outpouring might take a wholly unfamiliar form and bring with it certain radically new styles of piety. What seems more difficult to credit, however, is the contention that this amazing outpouring of grace—if authentic, one of the most remarkable in the entire history of the Church—should have the rather provincial locus that it has. Although the movement has become world-wide, not only its origins but much of its direction stems mainly from the American Middle West, in particular from two states (Indiana and Michigan) and more particularly from a handful of people who at one time were almost all associated with the University of Notre Dame. It is not difficult to believe that, like all movements, this one has grown out of a particular and unexpected kind of experience. The contention that this particular movement should be God's chosen way to renew his Church following the Second Vatican Council inevitably invites scepticism.

Is such a contention in fact made? Here as elsewhere the leadership of the movement seems studiously vague. A central question—is it God's will that all his people eventually become charismatics? —appears to be rarely candidly discussed. One early and prominent member of the movement insists that it is invalid to say, "It is not my cup of tea," since

the movement "is simply Christianity at its fullest."
To it, everyone is called.[13] One of its most influential
leaders says that the movement is intended by God
to renew the Church on every level.[14] They stop
short of insisting that all Christians ought to become
charismatics, but they also do not deny that propo-
sition, and the implication in its favor is quite
strong. Many ordinary charismatics seem in the
habit of referring to the movement as "the renewal,"
as though it were the only kind.

Put another way, are the charismatics willing to
admit that there are several forms of authentic Catholicism, and of authentic renewal of the Church,
that theirs is only one way, and that quite probably
it is not a suitable way for many people? There is
no evidence that the leadership makes any such admissions, much less that they ever actively discour-
age particular people from joining them, in the way
that religious communities have always discouraged
and if necessary rejected candidates deemed un-
suited for a particular way of life.

The very term "charismatic renewal" suggests the
problem, as does, in a slightly different way, the
term "pentecostalist." The word "charism" simply
means "gift," and it refers to those special gifts or
graces bestowed by the Spirit on individual Christians. In a sense every talent used in the Lord's service is a charism, although the word also has a more
particularized reference to gifts which are deemed
extraordinary, such as healing or prophesying.

When the movement of the past dozen years is

called "the" charismatic renewal, the unmistakable implication is that it has somehow cornered the Spirit's charisms. The leaders would probably not deny that people outside the movement (possibly even people critical of the movement) receive charisms, but neither do they affirm this possibility, and there remains a suspicion that they believe all or most of the Spirit's blessings are channeled through their movement. To call it pentecostalist is similarly misleading, because this implies that the outpouring of the Spirit on Pentecost is somehow confined to those who claim the name.

The obvious untenability of this position is immediately revealed upon recalling the life of that present-day Catholic who above all others is widely thought to practice heroic sanctity—Mother Teresa of Calcutta. There is no reason to think that Mother Teresa is a charismatic or is drawn towards that kind of piety. Should this be construed as an unfortunate failing on her part, making her example and inspiration less compelling than it might be? Surely the existence of various proven modes of spiritual renewal in the contemporary Church ought to make charismatics a bit more humble about asserting that their movement is destined by God for the renewal of His Church on all levels.

THE relationship of the movement to the regular hierarchical structure of the Church remains a very uncertain one, both on the theoretical and the practical levels. The most serious attempt to solve the problem—by reference to the apparent existence of unordained elders in the early Church and, a little later, of unordained monastic superiors[15]—is helpful but hardly conclusive, especially given the greatly more complex character of the present-day Church.

Perhaps the closest analogy for understanding Catholic charismatic communities would be religious orders. In both instances the individual is part of the larger Church but has also, for the sake of seeking a more perfect way, joined a particular community. Ordinary lay organizations like the Sodality are not comparable, because they do not encompass the lives of their members with anything approaching the totality of both religious orders and charismatic communities.

In the case of religious orders, however, the relationship to the hierarchical Church is well defined and carefully regulated. The order has a constitution and a rule approved by the ecclesiastical authorities. The rights and obligations of members are specified. In instances of grave disorder the bishop or, as a last resort, the Vatican can intervene. The approved rule of each community insures that the member's duties to the community never conflict with his or her duties to the whole Church.

No such safeguards appear to exist in the charismatic movement. Most charismatics belong to prayer groups which are somewhat loosely structured but which can sometimes have considerable impact on their members' lives. A significant minority, however, including virtually all of the leadership, belong to what are called "covenant communities." They live together in groups according to what amounts to a rule, and the covenant community dominates the lives of its members as thoroughly as does a religious order. (In this age of extremely lax religious disciplines, perhaps even moreso.) It appears that membership in a covenant community is held up as a kind of ideal for all charismatics.

In an age when formally constituted authorities are under frequent attack, power often passes to covert authorities who do not acknowledge having authority and are therefore not answerable for their decisions. In the charismatic movement the highest authority appears to be a group called merely a "service committee," whose members deny constituting any kind of hierarchy. How they are chosen and to what degree they are answerable for their actions is unclear. In practice, however, they appear to constitute a genuine hierarchy, with real authority over local communities. These local communities in turn have "heads" or "elders" who also appear to have genuine authority over the members. Almost all these people are laymen who have received no authorization from the Church, despite the fact that they often exercise authority in delicate areas involving consciences.

Occasionally a serious abuse occurs, such as at True House in South Bend, Indiana, where in 1974 it was charged that community leaders sometimes used dictatorial tactics upon members and applied methods of control which could legitimately be called brainwashing. The community was eventually dissolved, after admissions that serious mistakes of judgment had been made.[16] Later a prominent Notre Dame theologian, who had been deeply involved with the charismatics, also made criticisms about misuse of authority.[17]

The point here is not that such abuses may have occured in isolated cases. The history of practically all religious orders would probably reveal instances of abuse of this kind. Because religion penetrates so deeply into the human personality, it is always prone to fanaticism and perversion. The point is rather that the charismatic movement seems ultimately to have no structure of accountability within it. Whatever vigilance its leaders exercise is, apparently, unofficial and unspecified. Members of communities appear to have no guaranteed rights and no appeals to higher authority. (There are reported cases of members being told which priests they could go to confession to and which of their sins they could or could not confess.)[18] Bishops have no recognized right of visitation over local charismatic communities, nor do any international authorities, such as Vatican officials. Charismatic communities often seem to exercise strong religious discipline over their members, without being subject to any official ecclesiastical oversight.

The question is broader, however, than merely one of possible misuse of authority. This absence of ecclesiastical oversight raises the much more basic question of the charismatic movement's entire relationship to the Church, whether one of harmony, opposition, or separation.

A certain anti-institutional bias among some charismatics has already been noted. What is obvious among many "grass roots" charismatics is often less anti-institutionalism than obliviousness to and lack of concern for the institutional Church. What is real to such people is the presence of the Spirit in their own lives and the fellowship of the prayer group to which they belong. The Church as a whole seems to them like a kind of appendage, almost an irrelevancy. Most of them do not foresake their parishes (although some do), but their attachment to the institutional Church, in the line running from parish through diocese to the universal Church, seems merely a matter of habit—they were born Catholics, and most of them will remain Catholics. If popes and bishops support the movement, well and good. If they do not, the movement will go on under its own dynamic.

The movement can be praised for its success in rekindling a lively sense of personal faith in many people. The obverse of that success, however, is a faith so personal that everything outside one's own experience becomes unreal or unimportant. In their commendable concern that faith be living, not merely abstract, charismatics often seem to dismiss everything in the Church that they have not assimilated to their own piety. So strong is their sense of their own breakthrough in the spiritual life that, consciously or not, they seem to demean all other kinds of piety as retarded.

When charismatic piety becomes too intrusive, it also becomes divisive. There is no reason why prayer groups should not exist in every parish, if there are people who want them. However, if the charismatic form of piety is then imposed on the parish at large, especially if the priest himself affects a charismatic style in his preaching and liturgical celebrations, this cannot help but stir up confusion, resistance, and conflict. It is not reassuring to be told by the leading charismatic among the American bishops that when such resistance does arise it is probably due to "resentment" and even "envy" or that failure to accept the charismatic way requires "repentance."[19]

Ultimately the most basic question that must be asked of the charismatics is how they know that the promptings they experience are actually from the Holy Spirit, and what criteria they are willing to recognize as being applicable to such a judgment.

On one level this question returns to the charge of subjectivism which is sometimes levelled at them and which has already been discussed. The criticism here is not that charismatics espouse a highly personal and emotional piety but that they seem to lack any ultimate means of testing such a piety. Most charismatics appear to regard their religious experiences as self-validating, and outsiders who question these experiences are treated as merely unenlightened. Descriptions of the charismatic experience, especially in the early days of the movement at Duquesne and Notre Dame, seem like an emotional roller coaster—a constant succession of illuminations, personal breakthroughs, ineffable joys, temporary gloom quickly dispelled by minor miracles, sign upon sign, grace upon grace.[20] God might and probably sometimes has worked in such ways, but the charismatics come close, in many of their accounts, to claiming a virtual monopoly of divine power in their lives. (A key experience in the early movement was when the water supply at a retreat house failed, apparently necessitating the premature end of a charismatic gathering. When the water suddenly began to flow again, this was treated as a miracle and a sign of God's wanting the movement to continue.)

One of the charisms which has never disappeared from the Church is that of healing—many saints have been the instruments of miraculous cures through the centuries, and such occurences have not ceased even in the sceptical twentieth century. The charismatics, however, often seem to think that the power of healing is something they have rediscovered, and they imply that it is a power chan-

James Hitchcock

nelled primarily through their movement. Although
for years the Church has exercised vigilance over
miraculous claims of all kinds, such as the cures at
Lourdes, the charismatics seem to expect their own
claims of miraculous events to be accepted at face
value, and there is no indication of their willingness
to submit these and other experiences to the judgment of the Church. (There are close parallels, at
this point, between the charismatics and the Jansenists of the seventeenth and eighteenth centuries. The
Jansenists also preached a demanding kind of faith
amidst a culture which was self-indulgent and increasingly sceptical. They too claimed miraculous
events as a sign of their own authenticity. Although
continually protesting that they were loyal Catholics, they defied Church authority whenever it
sought to discipline them. It remains to be seen what
the charismatics would do in similar circumstances.)

The absolute conviction which many charismatics
have that their experiences really are the promptings
of the Spirit is one of the more disturbing aspects of
the movement, in the sense both that this assurance
reveals the absence of proper prudence and humility
and consequently a vulnerability to influences which
may not be divine at all, and that it betokens a misunderstanding of the spiritual life.

In the first flush of conversion it is understandable
that people are overwhelmed with joy and the sense
of the amazing abundance of God's grace in their
lives. However, long after this initial experience

many charismatics seem to continue to be on a perpetual "high." Their testimony about their condition heavily emphasizes the graces, consolations, even miracles they continually receive, the almost inexpressible happiness they constantly experience. They make people uncomfortable because of the suspicion that no one can be that happy all the time.

More is involved here than mere taste or personal style. Some charismatics seem to say that they belong to the movement because of the emotional consolations it brings and that the test of genuine spirituality is in those consolations. But the great spiritual teachers of Catholicism—people like Ignatius Loyola or Teresa of Avila—warn continually against mistaking consolations for authentic love of God. In fact they warn that an attachment to consolations is precisely a sign that one is a novice in the spiritual life and that many novices have been undone by the assumption that such consolations will and ought to continue indefinitely. Based on established Catholic criteria of spirituality it seems likely that many charismatics are indeed stumbling novices in the life of the soul but want to set themselves up as experienced teachers.

The emphasis on personal consolation has ecclesiological aspects also, again raising the question of the movement's relationship to the whole Church. Here the charismatics are not going contrary to the liberal and secular spirit of the age, for they seem to share in the general cultural assumption that "getting high" is a good thing. Like countless Catholics who have lost their faith since the Council, they assume that religion, in order to be valid, has to pack an emotional wallop. Their testimonies, often in an idiom borrowed from Protestant sects, are largely catalogues of moving experiences the individual has had.

The locus of most of these experiences seems to be either individual prayer or, more commonly, prayer meetings. Inevitably these "peak experiences" become the central realities of the individual's life. What then does this do to the Mass, which every Catholic ought to regard as the center of his or her life? Catholic charismatics profess that no problem exists here—they continue to participate in Mass, if anything with greater fervor than before. No doubt this assertion is sincere. However, how many Catholic charismatics can honestly say that Mass is really at the center of their lives, rather than the prayer meeting? Alternatively, there is a tendency to turn the Mass into a prayer meeting, something which is possible when all or most of the congregation are charismatics. A charismatic theologian who says that charismatics would not impose their style on an "unprepared" liturgical assembly[21] is not reassuring, since he seems to imply that such an imposition would be desirable if the assembly were in fact "prepared."

The central difficulty involves the act known as "baptism of the Spirit," the meaning of which is not agreed upon even by all charismatics. It involves a person's being prayed over by others in a group, who usually lay hands upon him and call down the Spirit. Often the person experiences a profound sense of the Spirit's having come upon him, leading to a total transformation of his life.[22]

Certain thoughts immediately come to mind: This act, ritualistic in character, seems to function almost as a sacrament, although it is not a sacrament the Church recognizes as such. It can be and usually is conferred through the instrumentality of laymen. The Church exercises no authority over its conferral. Most Catholics have never experienced it and in fact are even unaware of it. What then is its place in the life of the Church? Charismatics are again doubtlessly sincere in saying that in no way do they intend it as a new sacrament, much less as a rival to the existing sacraments. But in the reality of things it seems inevitable that it will occupy a central place in people's lives which the Church's sacraments do not have. A bishop, for example, admits that baptism and confirmation usually do not bring with them the lively sense that baptism in the Spirit brings and suggests that those who receive these sacraments lack "an expectant faith." Baptism in the Spirit is then defined as "prayer in expectant faith for a renewal of the sacraments of Baptism and Confirmation,"[23] which seems to mean that baptism in the Spirit is a necessary completion of the Church's sacraments, a contention which has profound and very disquieting implications for the whole sacramental life of the Church. (Certain obvious questions come to mind: Has Mother Teresa ever received baptism in the

Spirit? Has Pope John Paul II? Are they lacking something essential?) One admirer of the charismatics even talks about the widespread "failure" of the sacrament of baptism.[24]

Catholic spirituality has traditionally taught that tangible and lively experiences are not essential to the reality of faith, and it has been reserved in accepting the genuineness of such experiences. To a great extent the nature of sacramental piety dictates this reserve. It seems to be a point which many charismatics have not grasped.

The question of the relationship of Catholic to non-Catholic charismatics can now be raised once again, in a slightly different way. The problem is not that Catholic charismatics join in ecumenical activities. It is rather the question how far Catholic charismatics are committed to the Catholic Church, as distinct from their commitment to a movement which may eventually find the Church expendable.

It is ironic, in view of the frequent charge that Catholic charismatics are fundamentalists, to notice that liberal Protestant influence is not absent from the movement. One theologian, for example, seems to suggest that the Pentecost events may not have happened as described in the Acts of the Apostles but instead represent Luke's "editorial" use of certain data.[25] (Personal experience also confirms that some Catholic charismatics have imbibed the mentality of liberal Protestantism. The movement seems to provide them with an opportunity for religious commitment which bypasses troublesome questions about the authority and traditions of the Church.)

Claims that the Catholic charismatic movement is really Protestant do not come only from conservative Catholics. The following remarks are by a leading evangelical Protestant, following a visit to one of the leading Catholic charismatic groups, the Word of God Community in Ann Arbor, Michigan:

> . . . the Catholic charismatic element is clearly the nearest thing to Reformation Protestantism to come along in 400 years. It rivals the Jansenist movement of the seventeenth century, which stressed grace and was finally declared heretical.

> . . . they increasingly minimize the Roman Catholic features so strenuously fought by Protestants for four centuries. They could be called "crypto-evangelicals," meaning "evangelicals in disguise."

> The modern charismatic movement . . . has been able to suspend doctrinal questions and unite around a set of experiences. Doctrine divides. Experience unites.

> In the Word of God Community, I found doctrinal questions fielded graciously but with just a touch of annoyance, as if this kind of question is what sterile evangelicalism is hung up on. The agenda is more practical and immediate—the authority of elders, the place of prophecy in prayer groups and divine healing.

> Like so many other Catholic charismatics, Father Tickerhoof answered that the earlier sacramentalism in the history of the church was not *essentially* in error [emphasis added], but in the lives of many people it became an end in itself. It did not lead them to faith in Christ as it was intended.

He reported that what he has experienced in the
charismatic renewal achieved the goal of the sacraments
and, though they were still very important to him, there
was no confidence in the sacraments as such to achieve
salvation. . . .[26]

However accurate this outside impression (which
is intended to be sympathetic and favorable to the
Word of God Community), it is clear that Catholic
charismatics have many unresolved questions concerning their relationship to the Church and its traditions, and the future relationship of the movement
to the Church is by no means certain at this point.

It may seem unfair to raise the question, but at
some point it seems necessary to ask whether the
leading charismatics are in fact saints, as the Church
understands saints. The point of the question is sincere and is not intended to embarrass the charismatics. It is an important question because, whenever in the history of the Church God has inspired
things which were radically new and radically re-
newing, he has done so through the medium of particular saints. Great claims are made on behalf of
the charismatic renewal, but the nagging question
remains: Where does it get its authority, and how
can the authority be tested? While such judgments
are admittedly risky, impressions from outside suggest that the movement no doubt contains elements
of grace and divine inspiration, along with a powerful dose of human enthusiasm and commitment.
The signs of real sanctity, at least in any public and
visible way, are less easy to discern. There is much

sincerity, piety, and goodness. But in the end the outsider does not feel compelled to exclaim, "This is indeed from the Lord!"

The movement's problematic relationship to the larger Church gives rise to one final caution. It has already been noted that many people seem attracted to the movement because, almost alone, it appears to offer an intense and demanding kind of lived Christianity, at a time when indifference, laxness, even unbelief are rife. The danger is that the charismatic movement will drain off into itself a disproportionate number of those Catholics who are pious, devoted, and generous, who are seeking to be something more than routine Christians. It is perhaps a sign of the immaturity of the movement that for most charismatics it appears to be an end in itself. Those who join it become immersed in charismatic activities and are often lost to the larger Church. Many charismatics seem to conceive their relationship to the larger Church as being mainly one of proselytizing for the movement itself among other Catholics.

What Should We Think about the Charismatics?

TO use a popular colloquialism, the charismatics appear to be "on to something." What it is exactly is difficult to say, as all spiritual realities tend to elude definition. However, the charismatics have brought to the attention of the Catholic community certain elements of Christianity, especially a lively sense of the Spirit's workings and a corresponding sense of the personal lordship of Christ in people's lives, which have been neglected. They have furthermore discovered certain formulas which seem to "work," that is, they are effective in kindling a lively faith and especially in overcoming religious drift and confusion.

The problem, as discussed at some length above, is that the charismatics do not seem to know exactly what to do with their discovery. They are still so impressed with the power and the newness of it that they almost allow it to mesmerize them. They take their experiences as self-validating and do not subject them to sufficient testing and scrutiny. They seem to regard such experiences as ends in themselves, and much of their energy is devoted either to the movement itself or to proselytizing for the movement. Difficult questions concerning the sources of charismatic authority and the movement's relationship to the Church are not sufficiently probed.

Since there are no accurate statistics as to how many Catholic charismatics there are (such figures would be impossible to attain precisely, since belonging to the movement does not necessarily require a formal commitment), it is impossible to judge whether, in terms of numbers, it is increasing, declining, or stagnating. Certainly its popularity and its influence are still quite high.

It is realistic, however, to expect that within a few years' time it will begin to decline, in terms of numbers, influence, and visibility. Movements which depend so much on enthusiasm and deep personal involvement tend to go through periods of expansion and contraction since it is difficult for most people to sustain so high a level of zeal for very long. Many people are also swept along by the initial bursts of power but later lose interest or become disillusioned. (Intellectuals were, predictably, the first American Catholics to discover the charismatic reality and, equally predictably, are the first to express disenchantment, as William Storey and Josephine Massyngberde Ford have.) People who are searching for something often give themselves to a movement for a time, then find that it does not satisfy them and move on to other things. Finally, once a movement does begin to lose momentum, members begin to desert it in fairly large numbers, since many people's loyalties are governed by their sense of a movement's timeliness or apparent success. For all these reasons, once the charismatic movement begins to "peak," it will probably begin to decline fairly rapidly.

However, like the Church itself, the movement will decline from a rather high base, so that it will by no means disappear. Pockets of totally committed charismatics will survive and will have some influence. Perhaps more importantly, what might be called the charismatic style of spirituality will survive in the Church, even apart from an organized movement.

The key challenge facing the movement at present is to clarify and regularize its relationship to the Church at large. Primarily this should be done for the sake of truth. However, it would also be a process beneficial to the charismatics themselves, since it would help to place their spirituality on a firmer footing and, when the inevitable decline comes, it would help to cushion it, since the movement would then be an institutionalized element of the Church itself. (At present many charismatics give the impression that the Church needs them. The time may come when they need the Church even more. That time is in fact already here, although not recognized.)

It is not possible in a short space to specify all the ways in which the relationship of the movement to the Church should be regularized, and in any case a non-charismatic cannot undertake that task. However, a few general needs are obvious: Charismatic piety needs to be systematically evaluated by competent authorities as to the degree of its compatibility with Catholic doctrine. Extravagant claims for the movement—whether of tangible miracles like healing or less tangible spiritual blessings—should be advanced much more modestly and cautiously. A formal structure of ecclesiastical oversight needs to be established, in which lines of authority are clarified, rules are adopted, and powers of visitation and correction are vested in bishops and other appropriate Church officials.

In the end an authentically Catholic view of the charismatics is a quite simple one. The movement contains much that is good, valid, even perhaps necessary. Its continuing existence in the Church depends on the willingness of its members to accept the fact that they are a new and powerful kind of popular devotion, with all that implies. This means not only approval and review by the larger Church but also the recognition that charismatic piety is suitable only for some people. Tastes in devotion ebb and flow. (The great cult of Our Lady of Fatima, for example, so powerful in the 1950s, has all but disappeared.) If the charismatics can agree to be more modest and more humble about their claims, their movement may continue to irrigate the Church for a long time to come.

James Hitchcock

Notes

[1] See for example Josephine Massyngberde Ford, *Which Way for Catholic Pentecostals?* (New York, 1976).

[2] J. Kerkhofs, S.J. (ed.), *Catholic Pentecostals Now* (Staten Island, N.Y., 1977), pp. 20-1.

[3] Joseph H. Fichter, S.J., *The Catholic Cult of the Paraclete* (New York, 1975), p. 56.

[4] *Ibid.,* p. 114.

[5] *Ibid.,* pp. 53-5, 77, 90.

[6] See for example: O'Connor, *The Pentecostal Movement in the Catholic Church* (Notre Dame, Ind., 1971); Montague, *The Spirit and the Gifts* (New York, 1974); Gelpi, *Pentecostalism: a Theological Viewpoint* (New York, 1971), and *Pentecostal Piety* (New York, 1972); Tugwell, *Did You Receive the Spirit?* (New York, 1971); and McDonnell, *Charismatic Renewal and the Churches* (New York, 1976).

[7] Quoted in Kerkhofs, *Catholic Pentecostalism,* p. 62.

[8] Kieran Quinn, "Knox, Me, and the Pentecostals," *National Catholic Reporter,* Nov. 9, 1973, pp. 7-8. Orthodox Catholic critics of the Pentecostals should reflect that, with enemies like Quinn, the movement must be doing something right.

[9] Kerkhofs, *Catholic Pentecostalism,* pp. 49, 51-2, 61.

[10] Heribert Mühlen, "The Person of the Holy Spirit," in *The Holy Spirit and Power,* ed. McDonnell (Garden City, N.Y., 1975), pp. 31-2.

[11] Rene Laurentin, *Catholic Pentecostalism,* tr. Matthew J. O'Connell (Garden City, N.Y., 1977), pp. 54, 139-45. Although highly praised, this book is so naively credulous towards its subject that it could easily be used by the charismatics' critics.

[12] Montague, *Spirit and Gifts,* pp. 42-6.

[13] Patrick L. Bourgeois, *Can Catholics Be Charismatics?* (Hicksville, N.Y., 1976), p. 13.

43

[14] Kevin Ranaghan, "The Lord, the Spirit, and the Church," in *The Spirit and the Church,* ed. Ralph Martin (New York, 1976), p. 295.

[15] Stephen B. Clark, *Unordained Elders and Renewal Communities* (New York, 1976).

[16] See the *National Catholic Reporter,* Aug. 15, 1975, pp. 1, 2, and Aug. 29, 1975, pp. 4, 10. Although written by a hostile reporter, the essential accuracy of the articles has never been challenged. (A participant in the True House events has corroborated them for the author—J.H.)

[17] See interview with William Storey in *A.D. Correspondence,* May 24, 1975. It is impossible for outsiders to judge the accuracy of the charges and denials. However, the contention by charismatic leaders (*A.D. Correspondence,* June 21, 1975) that Professor Storey was uninformed about the nature of the movement hardly seems plausible, given the fact that many of the historical accounts of the movement mention him prominently. (See for example Martin, *Spirit and Church,* p. 12.)

[18] *A.D. Correspondence,* May 24, 1975.

[19] Most Rev. Joseph McKinney, in Martin, *Spirit and Church,* p. 104. Bishop McKinney is auxiliary bishop of Grand Rapids, Mich.

[20] See for example Paul and Mary Ann Gray, "God Breaks In," in Martin, *Spirit and Church,* pp. 11-20.

[21] Montague, *Spirit and Gifts,* p. 47.

[22] See for example Ford, *Baptism of the Spirit* (Techny, Ill., 1971). There are accounts of the phenomenon in Martin, *Spirit and Church,* and most other charismatic works, such as Kevin and Dorothy Ranaghan's *Catholic Pentecostalism* (Paramus, N.J., 1969).

[23] Bishop McKinney in Martin, *Spirit and Church,* p. 99.

[24] Laurentin, *Catholic Pentecostalism,* p. 41.

[25] Montague, *Spirit and Gifts,* pp. 27-8.

[26] Stephen Board, "Are the Catholic Charismatics 'Evangelicals?'," *Eternity,* July, 1978, pp. 12-6.

CATHOLIC PERSPECTIVES

Charismatics

PART TWO

by
Gloriana Bednarski, RSM

My deep gratitude, both for my understanding of the Charismatic Renewal and for their personal encouragement as I attempt to live it, must go to Sister Marina Kennedy, BVM, Matthew and Dennis Linn, SJ, Mrs. Barbara Shlemon and Peggy Kelly. For long hours spent in assisting me in clarifying my thoughts so that they might be accessible to those readers who are learning about the Charismatic experience through this book, I am equally indebted to Sister Julie Neal, RSM, and Sister Mary Ann Bender, OSF.

Gloriana Bednarski, RSM

Why I'm Writing about Charismatics

"YOU'RE going to a 'prayer meeting'? What is a sensible, well-educated person like you doing that for? With your solid background in theology, scripture, psychology, etc. etc. . . . ?"

Shouldn't I have known better? I was teaching at a progressive Catholic women's college at the time and giving workshops and seminars in the Chicago area and beyond in an effort to translate the excitement of post-Vatican II sacramental theology into new options for the people in the pews. There was fresh impetus toward a rejuvenated lay priesthood. The "news" was good and unique ministries were in the offing, and I was very enthusiastic.

Catholic ritual had been revised. Extreme Unction had become Anointing of the Sick. Confirmation now *could* renew a parish as the visiting bishop affirmed the Spirit of Jesus alive and well in its midst. There were rumblings of an entirely *re*charged approach to the Sacrament of Penance: that forgiveness could leave us not only sin-free but reconciled to one another. And fresh from the Vatican Liturgical and Sacramental Commission, a document entitled "The New Rite of Christian Initiation for Adults" held out the possibility of vast changes in the lives of our thousands of baptized

Catholics who certainly knew a great deal *about* Jesus Christ but, from all outward appearances, did not seem to have met him. Or so it seemed, since parish life as such did not, in many cases, generate energetic, *Christ*-ian communities that bore out our proudest claim: "By this shall all know that you are My disciples, if you have love, one for another" (John 13:35).

The teaching Church was, in that unusual moment of the mid-seventies, offering a totally different sacramental view but the Church in the pew, somehow, found it very painful to the traditional eye. The silence was deafening. And my disappointment was deepening as, from one parish to another, I spoke to small audiences—handfuls who could risk stepping into the light of the new vision that Jesus could be experienced in a different way.

Why the average twenty or thirty? I knew I was not an extraordinary believer. I was simply reaping the benefit of a vowed commitment to the Lord that placed me more directly into parish life and the study of theology. What was wrong, and why were so many parishes struggling against defection, apathy, and just plain boredom?

As I lectured and taught, I began to pray and hope that lay people would begin to grasp the power that *is* theirs as baptized, confirmed Christians— the power of their priesthood and the prophetic service that flows from it. It was the year 1974, that was how I felt, and that was what I perceived. And given the hugeness of the Chicago church, I was alone neither in my efforts nor my frustration.

The Risky Challenge

I had heard that a Charismatic prayer group was meeting weekly on our campus and, from the comfortably safe distance of my office, I watched its development with a peculiar blend of aversion, disdain, and out-and-out disbelief. To my own disadvantage, I kept a careful distance from this large group that called itself the Loyola-Mundelein Prayer Group and met in a building midway between these two institutions of higher learning—much higher, I remember thinking smugly, than what was going on in those strange meetings.

Although I am intellectually curious, I could scarcely fathom the notion of healing, prophecy, and praying in tongues going on in our day. Acts of the Apostles, yes! Today, no! And besides, "everyone said" that only emotionally unstable and somewhat unbalanced persons found their way there. In retrospect, I wonder at how readily I listened to critics from outside who had no personal experience from which to address this puzzling phenomenon with such disparaging conviction.

One evening, not out of curiosity but out of a genuine need for a deeper closeness to the Lord (in colloquial translation: things were going wrong for me and I needed God's help) I did go over to the meeting nervously, alone, and as anonymously as I could manage. Within minutes I knew I would not leave that group. Why?

There before me and around me was a genuine community at prayer, a microcosm of the Church with eight priests whom I knew and respected for theological expertise but never dreamed were involved in *this,* sisters (including a group of Cenacle sisters whom I expected to discern valid spirituality), and above all, over one hundred lay people of all ages with a significant number of young adults among them.

Something told me that this was what I had been searching for and working toward in the Church. And so I returned, week after week, to observe this incredible experience that these many men and women found to be quite credible. My problem— and it *was mine,* not theirs—with prayer in tongues, prophecy, and prayer for healing did not simply evaporate in one puff of smoke. (It occurred to me to say: "Holy Smoke," but I would not want to sound irreverent.) Preconceived biases and my concern for squaring these gifts of the Holy Spirit from Apostolic times with contemporary theological and scriptural teaching, spurred me on.

Gradually, one gift at a time, the soundness of it all struck me. Or, was it the Holy Spirit of Jesus that opened my eyes to understand what was happening? I began to desire not only these gifts of deep prayer and inner energy, but *whatever this was* that brought such a diverse group of individuals into what was the best effort to date at Christian community that I had encountered. I wanted that same experience of Jesus. I asked and learned from my new friends what I had not taught nor even learned in theology courses.

My faith in the charismatic gifts had to grow as, one by one, I came to value prayer in tongues, prophecy, and, most of all, the deep faith of lay people who prayed sincerely over the Word of God about the healing power of Jesus, took him seriously, and then stepped out in the faith that he would exercise this gift in our day through his believing people. "You will do the things I do, and far greater things than these" (John 14:12).

I had never taken his Word so seriously, and so I had not known his power so profoundly. I was deeply moved, and so I stayed—to learn from them.

How It Started: The History

"RENEW Your wonders in our time, as though for a new Pentecost," Pope John XXIII prayed in *Humanae Salutis* and that is how it all started. The Second Vatican Council opened the door of Catholicism and the Church discovered avenues not traveled for centuries. The Catholic experience of Pentecostalism which came to birth as the Charismatic Renewal was one of these avenues.

In January, 1967, a theology instructor at Duquesne University in Pittsburgh found his way to a Pentecostal prayer meeting in the home of a well-educated Presbyterian woman. He arrived there through a personal search that he and his colleagues had undertaken as they prayed over the Acts of the Apostles. Wondering at the powerlessness of their lives, they searched for a deeper awareness of the power and love of Jesus Christ's Risen Spirit in their own persons and in the Church. What Ralph Keifer discovered that first evening through "the laying on of hands" he carried with him to a unique weekend retreat in mid-February at Duquesne where thirty faculty members and students experienced the release of the Spirit of Jesus. What had been given them freely in their Baptism-Confirmation, they could suddenly sense in all its power.

These retreatants entered into a more immediate

experience of personal conversion—the Charismatic Experience in which one meets the Lord. Jesus stepped out of a *doctrine* and became a *person* with whom to walk through life. From Duquesne to Ann Arbor's University of Michigan to Notre Dame, this peculiar acultural religious phenomenon spread—not in factories and slums but in universities with students of theology whose background somehow allowed them to place this unique happening into a historico-scriptural perspective.

Prayer groups began to form, slowly and tentatively, as those who asked for this "release of the Spirit" received that for which they had prayed. They needed others who shared that same Experience with whom to understand, nurture, and grow into what was, at that point, startlingly extraordinary and highly suspect in the Catholic Church. Within these groups, unusual gifts became evident as amazed prayer groups began to see before their eyes shades of the Acts of the Apostles—prophecy, power in Scripture, dynamic teaching of the Word, healing, gifts of discernment, wisdom, knowledge, and that most puzzling ability to pray in tongues.

Where did these gifts come from? The *only* frame of reference for these first groups was the scriptural history of how the Holy Spirit revealed his presence in the early churches through these very charisms. And so, because these charisms resulted from their earnest prayer for personal renewal and renewal of the Church, they named it all the Charismatic Renewal. I remember Gamaliel's measure of validity and I observe that this must be a thing of God since it has not fallen under its own weight these twelve years. Perhaps the name is not as presumptuous as I once thought. (See Gamaliel, Acts 5:34-39.)

Initial suspicion on the part of the teaching Church evolved gradually into cautious approval as, interestingly enough, the official hierarchy never once thwarted the development of this new movement. Keeping a watchful eye is not synonymous with disapproval, and as the years passed, the mushrooming of prayer groups throughout and far beyond the United States called forth not a few official statements from national hierarchies of bishops. Conferences at Notre Dame seemed to be good yardsticks for annual growth from hundreds in the early seventies to tens of thousands by 1975.

Who attended these conferences? By this time, priests, sisters, bishops—and yes, Cardinal Leon-Josef Suenens! But, far and above all else, lay men and women. It was, without doubt, the largest lay movement in recent years. Pope Paul VI wanted a first-hand look and so invited the International Charismatic Conference to meet in Rome. He had already commented in an address to the cardinals of the Church in December, 1973: "The breath-giving influence of the Spirit has come to awaken latent forces within the Church, to stir up forgotten charisms, and to infuse a sense of vitality and joy." Any honest reading of his reactions to the 1975 Conference in Rome indicates Pope Paul's enthusiastic support and encouragement.

A solid theological study of how the Holy Spirit gifts his Church with charismatic power began to come forth from the minds and pens of Heribert Muehler, Bernard Haring, Rene Laurentin, George Montague, a very helpful Carroll Stuehlmueller, and a genuinely impressed Karl Rahner. With this invaluable contribution, the hundreds of prayer groups began to discern their place in the American Church.

Precious space need not be spent on much more history since, with the passing of years, the threat on both sides has subsided. An "apologia" is not really necessary. The bulk of our time should be spent on the theology of the Charismatic Experience, the strengths and weaknesses of charismatic practice today, and projections into the future of this renewal movement. For those seeking a more detailed background on the original Charismatic event and its development, *Catholic Pentecostals* (Kevin and Dorothy Ranaghan, Paulist Press: New York, 1969) remains the best treatment.

What Is Happening:
The Charismatic Experience
An Experiential Theology

IT is no longer premature to speak about a charismatic theology. Time and lived experience have permitted respected theologians to reflect creatively upon what has happened among charismatics themselves and in the Catholic Church as a result of their presence. It would seem natural that a set of unique terms would come into use much as occurred with the arrival of other theological schools of thought. I recall the controversy that swirled about many of Karl Rahner's concepts and am not dismayed at the misunderstanding that clouds refreshing insights with which charismatic theologians have enriched the Church.

"Life in the Spirit," "laying on of hands," "deliverance," "praying over someone," "Spirit-filled Christian," and more than all the rest, "Baptism in the Spirit," *appear,* at first glance, to be dangerously Protestant to the trained Catholic eye. But a careful, open-minded study of good charismatic literature reveals that these terms are solidly *sacramental.* It might be useful here to focus less upon their definition than on the starting point for all Christian experience—meeting Jesus the Lord.

Baptism In The Spirit—For a charismatic, "the Renewal" is not so much a weekly prayer meeting as the outgrowth of a deeply personal "experience,"

the Charismatic Experience of meeting the Lord in
a profound way. This "experience" transforms, frees,
opens individuals so completely to the power of the
Holy Spirit already given in their original and valid
Baptism and Confirmation that their lives are radically changed and redirected toward Church and
ministry.

The French have a more accurate term for this
Baptism in the Spirit. They call it the "release of the
Spirit." Quite simply, the power of the Holy Spirit
of Jesus and all that Jesus promised would be ours
as his ministers is released when I am confronted
with the Lord and *personally* choose to follow him
in whole-hearted, mature freedom. What needs to be
released in most adults is the power of their Baptism
and Confirmation, unrepeatable and unique moments of great gift, complete in that first giving but
received by us in infancy or childhood when the
depth of our response was certainly minimal at best.

At this point of *new life,* the experience of personal conversion often sends one to join others who
feel the same inner energy, and so prayer groups
form for the communal sharing of this deepened
faith, in prayer together *and* in ministry as a committed Church. Baptism in the Spirit, then, is a mature acceptance of Jesus as Lord and a renewed,
enlightened *re*-commitment to serve him more visibly
and consistently within the context of community
church.

The Gift of the Spirit—Relying heavily on Catholic
tradition, the renewed Christian responds to this un-

usual sense of life in the Spirit of Jesus with a spirituality of self-surrender. When once I know from the heart that the Indwelling Spirit is a reality for me, I surrender my natural giftedness and human weakness to the Lord who returns me to myself, my spirit transformed and my giftedness charged by the Gift of his Spirit. Isn't this what the Spirit of Jesus is? His own way of relating to people? Isn't this what the sacrament of Confirmation is? A deepening of the Lord's Spirit received in Baptism and taken on as a style of life in Confirmation?

What was Jesus' style if not healing, radical faith, prophecy, ecstatic joy in the Father, and discernment of his Will? What is Jesus' style in our day if not these very charisms operative in those who have experienced the release of his Spirit already given in their Baptism and Confirmation? This is why the term *Catholic Charismatics* came into use. It logically describes what is available to any and all Catholics—the charismatic gifts. Charismatics have never claimed an exclusive privilege to this baptismal birthright; perhaps, this suggests a need for greater awareness of what has been everyone's Gift.

Charismatic Gifts—Charismatic gifts are important and celebrated these days not because they are spectacular or bring some kind of distinction to individuals, but because these gifts are the channels of the Lord's powerful Word and touch for *the Body* —for anyone who needs them. A charismatic reverences the gift of *healing* not for personal aggrandizement but because it is a clear sign of Jesus' presence to his people in their need. Healing does not refer only to physical illness as many seem to think, but to inner unrest, wounded memories from the past, obsessive learned behavior such as fear, depression, unforgiveness—all of which block individual freedom *to be*—and finally, while rarely, possession that calls for deliverance. Healing is possible when a Christian, any Christian, surrenders to Jesus and is willing to be a channel for *Jesus* to reach out to someone who is suffering. This gift is based in part on the realization of the Apostles in Acts 3:6: "neither silver nor gold do I have, but what I have I give to you; in the Name of Jesus, be healed."

Often overlooked, the charismatic gift of *faith* steps out to heal and comfort with the confidence that Jesus' promise to ask and then expect to receive does hold even in our day. Not to be confused with intellectual assent to doctrine so important in its own right, this gift is an assent to the Person of Jesus and his powerful presence. Without this kind of faith there would be no healing. This does not differ theologically from current sacramental teaching which insists upon the readiness of *each* believer to rely on the personality of Jesus so as to touch others in seven healing ways. It should also be clear that *many* of us do exercise the gift of healing through charismatic faith and have done so for years. Charismatic theology helps us to pinpoint these gifts, grow in the awareness that they flow from the Holy Spirit given in Baptism, and expect to receive them personally.

Prophecy is cherished because the Word of the Lord is so indispensible to those who seek to live and serve as the Body of Jesus. Charismatic believers listen for the Lord as he speaks through members of his Body, thus directing the prayer of a group and, more importantly, their social outreach to those in need of ministry. Old Testament prophecy rarely revealed the distant future but most often challenged the day-by-day life and commitment of the people to Yahweh. Present-day prophecy should be understood in that same light.

Controversy and sheer disbelief surround this gift simply because it *seems* highly unlikely that God Himself would communicate so directly, so frequently, so indiscriminately in so many prayer meetings these days. That was my personal position until I heard Carroll Stuehlmueller's answer to a large group of priests and Scripture students three years ago. Since prophecy in Scripture is notably his area of lifelong study and expertise, he was asked: "What about the freedom of prophecy in charismatic prayer meetings? There is so much of it. How could it all be authentic?" My careful notes enable me to quote his response directly:

> Prophecy is the Word of the Spirit that brings to others the Will of God and the power to respond to it. This message enables the others to respond more fully *in a community way* (his emphasis). Each prayer meeting begins with strong, sustained prayer for the guidance and blessing of the Spirit of God and so there is an extraordinary sense of faith that the prophecy *is* under the Spirit

of God. There is a belief that this Word will have extra-ordinary effects in *this* community. My observation is that prophecy does shape the future of the prayer group because of the strong faith in it.

> (Mundelein Seminary Summer Biblical Institute, July, 1976)

My personal experiences over the years bear out Father Stuehlmueller's rather direct statement and compel my intellectual arrogance to give way to a humble acceptance of the reality that, when it comes to how God might choose to communicate, nothing is unlikely or impossible.

The Gift of Tongues—There is a real joy involved when we begin to realize and believe that the Lord moves and directs our lives even in their details and calls upon us to be his channel even through our weakness. To speak in tongues is to allow this joy to express itself more freely than were we to inter-ject human words. Scripture scholars look to Paul's teaching in Romans, Chapter 8:26-7 for a better understanding of this:

> The Spirit too helps us in our weakness, for we do not know how to pray as we ought; but the Spirit Himself makes intercession for us with groanings that cannot be expressed in speech. He who searches hearts knows what the Spirit means, for the Spirit intercedes for the saints as God Himself wills.
>
> (New American Bible)

Supported by this scriptural insight, charismatics allow the Spirit who lives within them to speak to the Father in words not intelligible to human ears, including their own. St. Francis' *Jubilatio,* well-known to Franciscans, and St. Teresa of Avila's comments on "praise that bursts through human limitations and ought not be stifled or ridiculed but cherished as a gift from God" are but two sources among others that indicate there has been a history within the Church of *prayer in tongues.*

My own history in regard to this particular gift remains for me a vivid example of how God's ways are not ours. I had no desire to pray in tongues and, to be truthful, I was somewhat put off by it. Yet, I well recall that the first time I heard our group of well over one hundred people singing in this strange but harmonious blend of as many languages as there were voices, I could not comprehend what was occurring but instinctively perceived without doubt that it was something sacred. Even so, I expressed my polite interest to the Lord about every other gift except this one. I remember praying as the weeks passed, not only to understand such things as prophecy, prayer for healing, and a more immediate knowledge and discernment of God's Will, but even to receive them. "Everything, Lord, except that gift of tongues. I really don't feel that I need *that* one."

Before long, however, I came to see that everyone around me in the prayer meeting would begin to praise the Lord and thank Him in English and reverently drift into those amazing indecipherable syllables. I knew they were praying and I envied how they could go on into extended praise beyond my few words in English. How many times can you repeat: "Thank You, Lord?" I ran out of words quickly. This was community at prayer and I wanted to join in.

As the realization dawned on me that I was missing something valuable, I began to intercede for even this gift: "Lord, I really wouldn't want to stand in the way if you truly wish me to pray in tongues." And, in time I did experience this unusual way of prayer so foreign to our Catholic style.

What gave me my purest understanding, though, was the situation in which I found myself at that time. Everything was wrong in my life, going from bad to worse: my job, a friendship on the rocks, my physical condition had thrust me into constant internal turmoil. Prior to my ability to pray in tongues, I could only come to the Lord in prayer, upset, hurt, angry, and asking him repeatedly: "Why? How could this be happening? Do something, Lord." Then, I found the Loyola-Mundelein Prayer Group and the Lord as well in my own, uniquely personal Charismatic Experience. The release of Jesus' Spirit that followed left me with the gift of prayer in tongues.

Suddenly I had a new prayer language, or as Paul put it, I had a new ability to allow the Spirit of Jesus, indwelling my spirit, to intercede to the Father, to praise him, to thank him. Incredibly, I found that I could go to prayer with the same agonizing problems and give them to the Father by way of this unique language. It isn't that I and my feelings were left out of my prayer. Rather, I somehow had learned to join my prayer with the Spirit's prayer, to permit him to assume my human burden and bring it to the Father with praise and thanksgiving since that is the language the Spirit speaks— *praise, thanks, glory.*

Humanly, *I* could not transcend my weakness and self-pity to praise God, even for these painful problems. But the Holy Spirit praying within me *could* and *did*. Only then did I grasp the beauty and value of the Spirit-Gift of tongues. The same gift that united frightened disciples into one magnificent prayer of praise at the Pentecost of a new Church made it possible for me in all my human brokenness, to surrender to the Spirit, to allow him to pray through me.

My initial objections about how educated, sensible people simply wouldn't babble uncontrollably gave way to a startling realization. One is not out of control when one deliberately puts the intellect to rest and gives the freedom to That which is in the depth of one's being to surge forth, the Source of a baptized Christian's very life—God's Breath. This is not unreasonable; it is a mystery—God's Love at work among us in yet another way.

Nowhere in Scripture is it written that this phenomenon of tongue-speaking along with the other charismatic gifts was to end with the passing of the Apostles. It hasn't. It has been necessary to devote a lengthier explanation to this gift primarily because it inevitably provokes more consternation, confusion, and even ridicule than almost anything else charismatic.

One of the predominant expressions of tongue-praying is the selfless praise of the Father which brings up yet another question. Why do charismatics walk around "praising the Lord" all the time? In a recent book, *Listening For the Lord* (Twenty-Third Pub.: West Mystic, Conn. 1977), I attempted to integrate charismatic spirituality within broad Catholic tradition and contemporary Church practice. Concerning the apparently incessant praise that characterizes many charismatics, for better or for worse, I can only quote:

> It is possible, given enough faith, trust, and love, to praise God in all things is to enter into a special way of loving Him. It is to love Him regardless of all that He can do for us. It is to surrender our wills to Him even if He were to do nothing for us. It is to give Him all burdens in trust without question of the outcome just as willingly as we worship in exuberant thanks for favors received.

> Praise is that prayer which touches a Father's heart because there is love for Him in the darkness as well as in the light. It is the prayer of the child who expects to receive of the Father's fullness and is content to leave that fulfillment to Him. For, one who truly praises, with no strings attached, has found that place within, that home of a special loving where the Revelation grows brighter with each day—that the Lord keeps us near Him and teaches us Love, praising Love.

Admittedly, cheerful "Praise the Lord's" can become a source of irritation. This was my reaction until I began to search more keenly behind those apparently worry-free faces. What I discovered, to my grudging admiration, was the maturing of *numbers* of contemplatives in blue collars who had come to experience the living God in reflective prayer. Overflow of encounter with Mystery is praise. I ceased my judgment and sought this unusual gift for myself.

Charismatic Giftedness, A Way of Life—But why is charismatic prayer so emotional, or at least why does it appear so? Charismatic gifts are for others, for the Body Church, for service in community and society. It would, indeed, be presumptuous to claim such gifts were they not nurtured through a lifestyle that maintains union with the Giver of their underlying power. To desire charismatic gifts as we have been describing them and as Paul identifies them in 1 Corinthians, Chapters 12-13, is certainly secondary and relative to knowing him and walking closely with him day by day so as to catch his Spirit. This is frequently misinterpreted by one-time, accidental observers at a prayer meeting, perhaps, because of the strangeness of it all. Could it be possible that what has appeared externally to be sheer emotionalism is, in fact, ecstatic joy in the union that genuine prayer is meant to prepare for? Could the Lord be *that* exciting? And could it be possible that occasional emotive prayer within community is a visible result of the daily, silent listening for the Lord that urges toward service in the normal mainstream of everyday life and the responsibilities that it entails?

What strikes one upon entering a prayer meeting is a prayerfulness that does not, at first glance, seem to be Catholic either in content or in style. Too much singing, too many different scriptural passages, too much exuberance—just too much for one evening. If one thinks that this is the prayer of merely one evening a week, then it *is* too much as well as inordinately bold to expect of the Lord all that charismatics ask in one prayer meeting.

In particular, one questions the claims to such delicately honed gifts as *knowledge, wisdom,* and *discernment.* However, in getting to know active charismatics personally, such questions dissolve into yet another awareness: that the richness of Catholic traditional devotional life has been revived and lives again in a rather large number of quite ordinary people. Without benefit of Jesuit training or even of qualified spiritual direction, countless Catholics have uncovered those beautiful prayer forms of the early Fathers of the Church, long cherished and at least tacitly reserved for the "holier ones" in our midst.

Ignatian meditation, *lectio divina* (the reflective reading of Scripture), the Jesus Prayer and its aftermath of contemplative prayer, and even an enlightened understanding and practice of the daily examen —all of these well known to priests, sisters, and a definite minority of lay people, have made the closer walk with the Lord available to any and every believing person.

No one would deny that other factors have had a part in the remarkable increase in the demand for spiritual direction, retreat opportunities, and even the evolving new roles of ministry within parishes. Those who have looked carefully at these trends admit, however, that an avalanche of lay charismatics thus far uneducated to deeper prayer and scriptural insight present themselves eagerly to those who will teach them. One is hard put to pinpoint any reason for this other than the Holy Spirit whose task has always been to inspire towards union with the Father, and actually effect it.

The lifestyle of the average charismatic *is* new and rearranged quite a bit. But is it actually new in the tradition of the Church? Is it against tradition to want a deeper life of prayer, a hunger for the Word of God in Scripture and for the sacraments, especially Eucharist, and want genuine need for shared faith in a Christian community with the growing ability to love and serve more freely and generously? All of this within the context of the same struggle with daily life problems that was always there but with a better perspective now on how to cope with them and one another.

Hasn't this been available to *all* Catholics? Certainly, yet if we have, at all, sought to make such a way of life our own, we admit that it is the person renewed by the Spirit of Jesus who can live it. Herein lies the strength of Charismatic Renewal—nothing really new nor different since the early Christian communities struggled with the gift of Baptism-Confirmation as we do today and learned to release *all* the power that was given them as children of God.

Those who have, by an accident of the Spirit, uncovered this hidden key to the remarkably effective
energy of early Christianity are only gradually
learning that charismatic giftedness is for *world*
renewal in the Spirit of Jesus the Lord. Catholic
sacrament intends to effect transformation in a
wounded society but its effectiveness is strangely
linked to the degree that society observes brothers
and sisters living in the oneness of a strong, communal witness.

As renewed people seek community, renewed
churches within parish form and proliferate throughout a diocese. Often, local pastors perceive the po-
tential energy for good and offer their support. Can
this be an example, just one, of Basic Christian
Community, American style? (Our version of "communidades de base," so important in Latin America
and Africa.) The strengths that the Charismatic
Renewal has provided to the Church are evident: a
deeper awareness of the holy life with the ability to
live it out more faithfully, the formation of strong
Christian community within the Catholic structure,
abiding concern for a positive relationship with the
teaching and authority of the Church, the endurance
to grow into a more pervasive and effective local
social ministry so as to influence society towards the
Lord's Gospel imperatives of peace, justice, and loving service.

Weaknesses In the Movement—As surely as the
strengths, there are weaknesses and, in some cases,

they are quite obvious. Fundamentalist biblical interpretation and poor teaching have plagued the leaders since the beginning. Yet it is only just to point out that Catholic scripture scholars and teachers kept a determined distance when hundreds of lay people, untrained in scriptural interpretation, discovered an insatiable hunger for Bible Study. The arrival of increasing numbers of well-prepared Catholic teachers has short-circuited faulty teaching, i.e. witness several major universities like Loyola of Chicago and St. Mary's of San Antonio offering ongoing, college-level training programs specifically geared to the needs of leaders in local prayer groups. The problem is subsiding.

What was once a weakness, the poor social outreach of prayer groups, is now evolving into more consistent action than most parish efforts to date can demonstrate. (More about this later on in this text.) Having touched upon emotionalism, I would only suggest that as charismatics become more accustomed to the "Experience" and the enthusiasm that follows upon it, they find it possible to temper their occasionally over-zealous desire to share what they have found to be so very good. What can one say except that we could do worse than get excited about Jesus. Excessive piety and perpetual smiles are, nevertheless, hard to endure, but with maturity will come balance, as in all honeymoons, that must eventually grow into a deepening joy.

Another often cited weakness is the dangerous ecumenism that charismatics reportedly expose themselves to as they mingle with other Christian churches more freely than before. What brings us together is the central focus on Jesus the Lord. What keeps us apart is the continuing inability to share Eucharist. For each citation of the dangers that this closeness *could* incite, I would have to insist, in all honesty, that I have witnessed greater caution over the question of intercommunion in charismatic gatherings large and small than has been my experience on campuses and in other non-charismatic situations.

An event that has made an indelible impression on anyone who attended it, whether participant, press corps, or skeptic, was the 1977 Conference on Charismatic Renewal in the Christian Churches. From July 20th through the 24th, Kansas City teemed with an estimated 55 thousand Pentecostals from the Baptist, Episcopalian, Lutheran, Mennonite, Presbyterian, United Methodist and non-denominational traditions. This included the original Pentecostals and a clear majority of Catholic Charismatics. The presence and public teaching of Cardinal Suenens and a number of Catholic bishops and the fact that this huge undertaking was organized, in large part, by the National Catholic Charismatic Service Committee from Notre Dame assured anything but dangerous ecumenism.

At once a drawback and strength, we experienced the reality that sharing the table of Eucharist was not yet possible. Respectful of this problem, separate meetings were held in the mornings to provide strictly denominational teaching and Eucharist. Afternoon sessions were set up to welcome and instruct us in one another's differences as well as unifying factors while we visited one another's workshops. Only in the evening did the entire conference come together for praise, thanksgiving, interfaith teaching, and witness.

What memorable evenings they were. We were proud of our hierarchy when they taught, witnessed, shared Catholicism with the assembly and truly were impressed with the sincerity of belief that our brothers and sisters in other churches held out for our understanding. Above all else and at the center of this first-ever ecumenical endeavor on such a massive scale was the commitment of tens of thousands of people to Jesus the Lord. No breaking of church law, no intercommunion. Just a fleeting foretaste of what must yet come to pass since Jesus prayed for it: "That they all may be one, Father, as You in me and I in You, that they all may be one in us" (John 17:21).

Again, is not shaky ecumenism experienced by the entire Catholic Church, a problem that ought to be approached more practically by focusing on stronger Catholic witness at all levels of Church life? The defections I know of result from weaknesses in institutional Catholic parish life that forced sincere people to turn away to where the Spirit of Jesus was more evident.

Turning in another direction, we know that much study and guidance is needed in regard to the practice known to charismatics as *prayer for deliverance* and known to many others as *finding a devil around every corner*. This problem relates directly to non-Catholic teaching that early charismatics swallowed totally from preachers of other Christian traditions and will only be corrected as Catholic theologians roll up their sleeves, look seriously at the question of evil in this world, and reinterpret this presence within the Catholic context. Charismatics are not *entirely* wrong on this! Karl Menninger's book, *Whatever Happened To Sin?* warned us some years back that we were giving too much leeway to evil. Whether in its personification as "demons" or not, the subject is increasingly urgent and must be addressed. Work by Rev. George Maloney, S.J. and several others has opened the subject and their very genuine case studies will convince the skeptic.

If it seems that I have been excusing charismatics for their weaknesses, I have, to some degree. The Church *is* charismatic, gifted with Jesus' personality. It always has been. The sooner everyone realizes that we are here to stay and accepts our weaknesses along with our very real strengths, the sooner these problematic areas can be treated and corrected.

What is happening with charismatics? The experience of Jesus has become a greater reality for them than they ever imagined possible—a genuine *lay* movement of a greater scope and power than the Catholic Church has known in centuries, a movement that refuses to be the *fad* that everyone was sure it was. With the experience came the strengths, the weaknesses, and some interesting prospects for an even more powerful future. At thirteen years of age, there is promise of much to come!

Further commentary and research as to charismatic theology can be found in:

Suenens, Leon-Josef, *A New Pentecost?* (Seabury Press: New York), 1974.

———, *Ecumenism and Charismatic Renewal: Theological and Pastoral Orientations* (Servant Pub.: Notre Dame), 1978.

Rahner, Karl, *A New Baptism in the Spirit: Confirmation Today* (Dimension Bks.: Denville, N.J.), 1975.

Muhlen, Heribert, *A Charismatic Theology: Initiation in the Spirit* (Paulist Press: New York), 1978.

Malines Document, *Theological Pastoral Orientations on the Catholic Charismatic Renewal* (Servant Pub.: Notre Dame), 1974.

McDonnell, Kilian, OSB, *The Holy Spirit and Power: The Catholic Charismatic Renewal* (Doubleday Press: New York), 1975.

Where It Is Going: Future Trends

Charismatic Community and Social Outreach

FROM the beginning, one of the guiding principles by which charismatic prayer groups formed and lived was the firm belief that they would not long remain distinct from their local parishes, but would, in fact, be integrated into them. National leaders expanded this conviction into a goal: that eventually the Charismatic Renewal would disappear into the Church. With some clarification, what might appear quite presumptuous does become acceptable and, perhaps, even desirable at this point in the history of the American Catholic Church.

There is a growing consensus that trends in society these past years have confronted our "one, holy, catholic, apostolic church" and found it more than a bit lacking in unity, holiness, and single-hearted service to all of the people of God. The divorce rate, corruption in professional practice, decline of Christian moral values, to name a few—all abound with high incidence among Catholics. We can only mention in passing the valid observation that a lifelong vocational commitment to the Lord becomes increasingly difficult for many with each passing year. The marks of the Catholic Church are dusty lately, not nearly as prominent and beautiful in our lives as they once were.

Is it possible that the Holy Spirit is giving his special gifts to the entire Church at a time when we most need them—his charisms uniquely designed to restore and maintain oneness, holiness, and genuinely Catholic (open to all), apostolic witness *now?* Discernment, healing, radical faith, prophecy, and the wisdom to listen to it—we need these gifts not only to elucidate for us the marks of our church as it must live in contemporary culture but to fill in the cracks in the structure and policies of a Church that is not always successful at being one, holy, catholic, apostolic, and (remember the rest of the definition recited by every Catholic child) guided by the Holy Spirit.

What could we expect as a church today if we took the guidance of the Holy Spirit through his charisms seriously? What forms might our giftedness take these days and would the contemporary church be open to responsibility for self-surrender to Jesus the Lord that charismatic giftedness entails? Our only source for adequate understanding, once again, is the history of those small churches first gifted in this way, the Christian churches described in the Acts of the Apostles. As I study the first four chapters of the Acts, I ask myself: "Who is living that way today?"

The Acts teach us about *community* and the gifts required for the formation of strong communities; about *healing* and the gifts and attitudes that allow for Jesus' healing to continue in His Church; about *justice* and the gifts indispensable for the kind of

76

social outreach that transforms oppression into ful-
fillment in the Christian context. Charismatics are
learning a great deal about community, healing,
social outreach, and the power of charismatic giftedness that makes them happen. What is happening
can be invaluable towards strengthening the Church
in its struggle on the contemporary scene.

To learn is not to be perfect. Charismatics have
only begun and at times we do poorly at best. But
the Holy Spirit is a patient teacher. The question is
not whether the Spirit wills to "do a new thing" in
his Church today but whether the Church will accept the challenge of his powerful gifts. Power is
always a serious risk that must be taken when it
arises and translated into renewal. Does the Church
want to be a healing, just community in the manner
of Jesus Christ? Then it will need the charisms that
lend the power of the Risen Lord toward personal
and communal renewal. This is what is meant by
charismatic renewal becoming part of the life of the
church in our day. Nothing more, nothing less. No
one excluded in any way. And we are only just beginning to understand it.

Community—Every variation of community exists
on the American scene as people cluster together
around causes, convictions, beliefs, and lifestyles.
Many begin with the promise of vigor and a future,
have a short life-span and dissolve. Others continue
and seem to gain momentum as they develop. The
dispassionate critic might observe that, though every

community must cultivate its existence through a phase of intense self-nurturing, some never pass out of this into an other-centered style of life. In essence, groups that remain fixated on their own identity refuse to move out of the womb of a warm security and die a social still-birth, while groups that allow the creative energy that their fellowship has generated to reach out in a life-giving, person-sharing plan of action, thrive and mature into significance beyond their expectations.

One definition of Christian community under the direction of the Holy Spirit might put the emphasis in this way: a community that allows the energy and grace of its fellowship in the Name of Jesus the Lord to reach out will renew its parish, neighborhood, society, simply by generating for others what it is experiencing itself day by day. Within this type of church to be *community* is to be *healing* and *just.*

Charismatic community evolves in a scenario something like this: An individual whose life has become difficult, stressful, at best meaningless, meets up with someone whose life speaks of peace within stress and a sense of purpose and meaning. Liking what he sees, he becomes acquainted with his new friend's style of life, values, and community. There he comes up against an environment of healthy relationships centered around the Person Jesus. In the delicate gentleness that sometimes characterizes an encounter with the Lord, he comes into his personal conversion and is born into life in Jesus' Spirit as well as life in the community. As he begins to nurture this conversion into maturity through his sharing in community life, so the community nurtures its fellowship through the charisms of Jesus' Holy Spirit, always straining toward a maturity that will allow the giftedness of the members to reach out ever more and more in gentle strength of witness through action. As the community serves whatever need within the neighborhood, it grows into a keener sense of justice and peace. Only, this time the mission is empowered by the Lord's Spirit and the customary burnout of valiant but dead-end individual efforts toward transformation of social ills is avoided.

The difference between activist and apostle becomes more evident and the social injustices and needs become more immediate. Close-to-home problems of those neglected in any way down the street and in the parish become the *starting* point for discerning a community service and concentration on these local situations will demand enduring commitment and long-term personal follow-up. Collections for overseas missions will remain important but involved, consistent, loving ministry will be geared to the poor, sick, elderly, jobless, addicted, alienated family next door and down the road.

The thrust here is *involved, consistent, long-term, personal.* Should the reader be questioning this scenario with raised eyebrow and the mildly defensive comment that many Catholics do this kind of thing all the time, let me hasten to add two further comments. First, indeed many Catholics have taken on an individual, often uniquely personal dedication to one or another of the social ministries, so much so that they stand out in the crowd as owners of a special charism. What charismatics are learning is that, perhaps, the Spirit can gift an entire community, many communities with an energy of love for one another so strong that Catholics will not hesitate to reach out precisely *as* communities that are agents for social change.

Since the Charismatic Renewal is primarily a lay movement, we might look beyond religious communities of sisters, brothers and priests in this discussion. Quite often, the very existence and work of these "professionals" in the Church has tended to exonerate many members of "the rest of the Church" from enduring commitment to service outside the home. Colloquially speaking, didn't this mentality "let us off the hook"? My second comment is brief: that many wealthy parishes do "twin" with poor parishes. Yet it is the exceptional situation where personal involvement and sharing of life between the two occurs beyond the contribution of surplus wealth.

The Pentecostal experience came into the Catholic Church with a unique focus upon *community,* quite different from its focus on individual piety in the Protestant understanding of being *born again.* With this gift of community (and the ability to form community *is* gift beyond any human design alone), came the power of the Holy Spirit to be shared within a community henceforth to overflow into a more *enduring* work for justice—a transformation of unjust systems and structures through the Lord's power at work in His Community. This is the Incarnate God at work and Incarnation is an important part of Catholic doctrine. Incarnational spirituality assures less burnout and more stable servant love.

There are more than enough examples of how this expresses itself within the Charismatic Renewal. One might image a transfusion of the Lord's dynamic Love, channeled through the members of a community, one to another, and then, outward to those people who most need that same love, and back again into community—a movement of life and healing both among and outward, stimulated and sparked by the Word of God in Scripture and the healing touch of Jesus in the sacraments.

Those acquainted with Latin American spiritual life will recognize in this particular mix of religion and work for justice, the development of a community model extraordinary in our time: "communidades de base," *basic Christian community.* The Latin American Documentation Service defines them thus: "small groups of believers—much smaller and more localized than the typical parish—who pray, study their faith, and share a common Christian life together" (LADOC Keyhole Series, no. 14, p. 2).

In this approach, the community simply exists, trying to take concrete steps in faith in the context of real life circumstances. This walk in faith has become so powerful that, in present day Latin Amer-

81

ica, mighty governments fight to eradicate over *one hundred fifty thousand* of these base communities because they are a serious threat. The Word of Scripture and the grace of sacrament heard and celebrated in community have charged simple people to challenge their own oppression with the power of God.

I experienced this first-hand when I was one of twenty-six Americans invited to dialogue with Latin American community leaders in the Inter-Continental Charismatic Social Justice Conference that was held in Scottsdale, Arizona, in December of 1975. There I met unforgettable men and women from Mexico, Colombia, and Central America and listened to stories of how the Spirit worked in their communities.

Monsignor Carlos Telaveras of Mexico City described the plight of a large number of squatters who lived in the garbage dump on the edge of an airport outside the city. When the Mayor ordered their eviction because of a future expansion project at the airport, these fragmented peasant folk took several simple steps. First, they sought the Lord together in prayer and he gifted them with the unity they needed to become a community. Then, they began to help one another with the meager funds they had, sharing everything and gathering together around the Word of Scripture. As they did this, their awareness of themselves as people with basic human rights grew and their sense of purpose united them in strength. Now a strong community, they made

a personal, formal protest to the municipal authority and thoroughly shocked the mayor. Recognizing
that this was no longer a divided, powerless rabble
crowd before him, he was forced to reconsider the
entire project. The final decision saw pre-fabricated
housing built for the Squatter Community and its
members put to work on the airport expansion
project. This is a vivid case history of a group that
worked out a program for community life together
in which their faith in Jesus Christ was integrated
into political-social action that made possible their
freedom to live and love and grow as families in a
humane way.

There were many more stories and the challenge
from this conference was real. The Latinos asked
pointed questions four years ago: What happens to
your neighborhoods and your families because of
your prayer groups? Does your human life and the
spirit in your area grow in holiness because your
prayer group meets there? Is *anything* changing in
your work and daily situation outside the community? If not, why are you meeting? Why is this Charismatic Renewal in America not making a social
impact?

The end of the nurturing phase was upon us here
in the United States and we knew it that week in
Scottsdale. The security of a sheltering community
needed to give way to the urge for outreach to heal
crippling injustice and the suffering of our own dis-
advantaged people. American charismatic prayer
groups heard the strongest challenge to date at the

1976 Notre Dame Conference when Father Michael Scanlan, then leader of the American movement, insisted that social concern for and personal sharing in the plight of oppressed brothers and sisters was to be every community's agenda and that the power of the Holy Spirit would be there to carry this out.

Oppression wears as many hats as there are people who need healing. Local prayer groups throughout the country reassessed the quality of their life together and began to test the climate out in the neighborhoods and parishes. The time seemed ripe for pressing charismatic gifts into service for others. Ordinary lay men and women rolled up their sleeves, read the signs of the times, and saw that the sacred moments of the prayer meeting did, in fact, empower them for action in society.

This was the season when countless Vietnamese refugee families were adopted by charismatic groups and integrated into American life through their ongoing assistance. Prayer groups learned that they could do more than pray together. They applied for green cards and food stamps, sought out apartments and employment, offered stability and friendship in a strange land. Three years later, these same prayer groups are once again opening their communities to the Indo-Chinese boat people and assisting them in the same way.

In early 1976, the Loyola-Mundelein Prayer Group on Chicago's north side began to reach out to the physically handicapped shut-ins. Once a month, drivers gathered the disabled from many sections of the city. We celebrated Eucharist with them, socialized and ate with them, introduced them to one another. Three years later, these handicapped people have learned to reach out to one another's affliction and loneliness with the compassionate companionship that can only come from having shared one another's experience.

One about-to-retire member of the Loyola-Mundelein Community decided to do more. Rosemary Koenig knew that the physically handicapped needed a community more than once a month and has set out to purchase a home where a small group can live and to which others can come for assistance. "The Shelter of God's Love" is in the planning stages but prospective residents are ready and waiting and volunteer workers are in the wings as Rosemary collects the rather large downpayment in dribs and drabs from charismatics throughout the city.

Yet another team of lay ministers of Communion from this college-based prayer group began in 1976 to establish base communities in halfway houses for recovering mentally ill people who had been released from large mental institutions. Thousands of these abandoned people live in one sprawling psychiatric ghetto in Uptown Chicago, with little or no pastoral care or social outreach ever touching them. Three years later, seven lay ministers are working in eight halfway houses to develop Christian communities centered on the Word of God and the sacrament of Jesus. Very gradual but genuine signs of healing and self-determination are becoming evident in this basically chronically schizophrenic population. These neglected people share the neighborhood with the Loyola-Mundelein Prayer Group and so we share our charismatic giftedness with them.

A few years back, Loyola-Mundelein would have been considered exceptionally active beyond its weekly Thursday night prayer meeting. Today, the examples just given are duplicated and augmented by a diversity of ministries throughout the Chicago area. And word from charismatic groups in other parts of the country only confirms the growing social awareness of most charismatic communities. The level of personal contact with those to whom we minister and the ongoing commitment that is usually required cause me to pause and wonder why charismatics are so frequently accused of social ineptitude.

It would be closer to the truth to acknowledge that, perhaps, the *local prayer group-growing into community-reaching out to serve* is far more effective psychologically and spiritually than perennial efforts in huge parishes to fulfill social needs without a community of individuals who are willing to involve themselves personally in social ministry. Experience in social action has proven that people need to be sustained within a nurturing community if they are, in turn, to sustain the draining demands of social ministry. This is, after all, a prophetic role— attempting the transformation of oppression into the freedom to live and love.

Today's charismatic prayer groups are still learning to live community with an eye toward social change. That they have given time, even years, to nurture the Word of God and his Eucharistic Presence in their midst is not at all an indication of weak-kneed navel-gazing. Without the Lord, there is no power! That they shall grow out of this important developmental phase into a realistic, empowered building of the Kingdom of God in our highly secular cities is a Word they are now beginning to hear and to heed.

In the final analysis, it ought not disturb us too much that charismatic prayer groups have dwelt a while longer on the fundamental realization of the followers of Jesus, "He who lives in me and I in him, will produce abundantly, for apart from me you can do nothing" (Jn. 15:5). The genuine disaster of this age in the Church may well turn out to be the best-planned but ineffective programs and projects of sincere Christians who set out to conquer injustice, whether systemic or personal, without having listened carefully nor long enough to the heart of Jesus the Lord: "If you live in me and my words stay part of you, you may ask what you will, and it will be done for you" (Jn. 15:7). (For further reflection and suggestions on this subject, see *Charismatic Social Action: Reflection/Resource Manual,* by Sheila Fahey (Paulist Press: New York), 1977.

Healing—Christian community centered around Jesus, his Word, and his sacraments is seen by theologians to be *in itself* all that is necessary for the work of justice. Jesus has promised the power needed for societal renewal to those who believe in him:

> "I solemnly assure you, the one who has faith in me will do the works I do, and greater far than these. Why? Because I go to the Father, and whatever you ask in my Name, I will do (Jn. 14:12-13).

What the Lord holds out to us as the task of justice is the ability to achieve a transformation of far-reaching consequences—no less than the healing of individuals, families, churches, and nations if we will accept the charismatic giftedness to heal in his Name.

Scripture integrates the gifts of the Spirit of Jesus for those who will attempt to understand them in the midst of contemporary culture—a culture which would raise up scientifically grounded materialism as the only certitude in human life to the exclusion of spiritual reality. The teaching of Jesus clearly links the gift of *radical faith* in his Word with the gift of healing: "I give you my Word; if you are ready to believe that you will receive whatever you ask for in prayer, it shall be done for you" (Mark 11:24). What stronger emphasis can he place upon both his consuming desire to reach out to his suffering people to bring them wholeness and his intention to accomplish this through disciples who will be open channels for his grace and power? Is this not yet another aspect of Incarnational spirituality?

Traditionally, Catholics have prayed to be the Lord's feet to carry him where He would wish to go and his hands to touch those who will perish without his comfort. Is it not one small step further in this association of images to understand ourselves as ministers of Jesus' healing? "Live on in Me as I live in you" (Jn. 15:4). And yet, a major stumbling block for many religious people today is precisely this: that Jesus the Lord intends to heal physically, psychologically, spiritually, in our time through the channel of those who will be conduits of the most effective agent of healing this world has ever known—the saving love of his Father.

It is not a question of worthiness but of willingness in the face of true *un*-worthiness. It is not a process of one-shot tent healing but of a gradual turning toward Jesus through the patient encouragement of a friend who will lead, minister, "stand under" the power of the Spirit, and "live" sacrament with someone who has looked to God for healing. This is the Catholic way, not sensational or hyperemotional, but enduring and communal. Willing to wait for the Lord, but with a new expectation: that the Anointing of the Sick is a sacrament that *can* heal, that Eucharist *will* heal, that the Sacrament of Reconciliation *is* healing in the forgiveness that releases pain. All of this ought to be expected because the sacrament received *is* Jesus and Jesus heals.

The Catholic Church has always taught that the sacraments are visible, authentic avenues for the new life that Jesus offers when he meets a needy person who believes in him. In our lifetime, we have looked more deeply into the often quoted truth that nothing is impossible for God, and dared to take it all the way to whatever healing Jesus intends, rather than limit him by what seems possible to us in a given situation.

Charismatic prayer groups had no more preparation for this extraordinary phenomenon than any other group in the Church. The Spirit prompted the early charismatics to pray with those who sought healing and healing occurred. It seemed quite as incredible to them as it might to anyone outside the movement, and self-knowledge indicated to those who perceived that they were gifted in this way, that, without doubt, it was not they but the Lord Jesus at work.

As Catholics are inclined to do, charismatic ministers of healing began to veer toward prayer for healing within community. Through the solid and remarkable experiences of Barbara Shlemon, a nurse, mother, and housewife, Sister Jeanne Hill, a Dominican sister, Father Paul Schaaf, a Precious Blood priest, and others, charismatic groups throughout the country and on into other countries as far as India and Australia, learned about *soaking* sick persons in prayer within the community in which they shared life. This is an ongoing, frequent, and patient process by which *many* can offer the support, love, and powerful prayer that not only channels Jesus' healing to the sick member but often heals any disunity, strife, difficulty among those who unite in the prayer.

Experienced teachers like Fathers Matthew and Dennis Linn, S.J., and Father Michael Scanlan, president of Steubenville College, provided more and more sound approaches to inner healing through the *healing of memories* grounded carefully in the psychology of the human personality and the best of insights from the "death and dying" movement in this country. Father George Maloney, S.J., an expert in Eastern spirituality, provided the balance so sorely needed in the area of *spiritual discernment,* weaving a path of sound teaching through some of the distortions regarding "deliverance from demons" and occult practices that had been confusing to the lay person.

What has emerged as a result of twelve years of rich experience and insight from these profoundly religious and balanced sources is a wide range of possible approaches to the various areas of healing through prayer, Scripture, and sacrament, within the support system of community. It has become clear that the resources of the Church are more than able for the physical, psychological, and spiritual healing of its people—all can be healed if opened to the Spirit of Jesus.

Nearly as important as the gift of *healing* is the attitude that must accompany it. "Lord, I am not worthy, but only say the word and I *shall be* healed." Those who pray for healing and the one seeking it place themselves in a stance of simple, expectant faith, knowing that Jesus is the one who heals, and that he also knows the specific healing, whether physical, inner, or spiritual that is most immediately needed.

Just as the medical profession is coming to grips with the discovery that at least 80 percent of all physical illness is psychosomatic in origin, at least to some degree, the charismatic gift of healing is making good on Jesus' command in the face of Lazarus' death: "Untie him and let him go free" (Jn. 11:44). The Lord consistently asked for the faith that expected healing. And that is *all* he requested. Is it not strange that those who seek healing from him in expectant faith and receive it, both those who pray for the healing and the one who seeks it, are often looked upon with distrust and mild ridicule?

That God is the source of this remarkable and persistent charismatic gift must become more evident when we notice that those who found it most difficult to accept the possibility of healing through faith have come around to less skepticism and more serious study. Physicians, nurses, psychiatrists, counselors, social workers are at the least more cautious in their criticism while, at best, seeking to integrate prayer for healing with their practices in a responsible manner.

In August, 1975, 32 health professionals met at Mount Augustine Retreat Center on Staten Island, New York. In that meeting, the Association of

Christian Therapists was founded "to promote the healing power of the Lord, helping people toward wholeness and holiness through healing prayer." Its formal purpose deals an educated death blow to the dichotomy between faith and medical care:

> ACT is all embracing in the healing disciplines; it represents a community of faith; it speaks of healing. Its aim is not to replace traditional medical practice or technology with prayer, but to integrate the dimension of prayer into the healing profession. Members benefit from shared prayer and personal ministry, acknowledging their own woundedness and willingness to meet the needs of another. (stated Purpose, ACT bylaws)

Since that first historic meeting four years ago, membership has mushroomed to over 600 professionals from as far away as Canada and Hawaii representing every known specialization. This extraordinary growth shows no indication of letting up and over 20 geographic regions in the United States are in process of formation. Two national conferences each year bring the members together for a truly unique opportunity to learn from one another's experiences as well as from the founding healing team.

In the light of all that has been presented, it should not be necessary to mention that the only qualification for the ministry of healing through faith is belief in the power of Jesus' Spirit as he makes it available through prayer, Scripture, and sacrament within any community church that is open to be a channel for his healing, wherever someone needs it. One might, therefore, anticipate with confidence that other professional groups might join together to discern, pray over, and move with healing into their specific milieux. We think of thousands of dedicated teachers in the numerous branches of education, politicians, executives, as well as employees engaged in sales or public transportation services.

If this question of healing through faith is somehow objectionable because it is related to the development of the Charismatic Renewal in the Catholic Church, then, with all haste, let us disengage the two. The healing that Jesus means to give his people has always been available for the asking. The fact that it is happening with greater and greater frequency these days must indicate that the majority of Catholics may have underestimated both the Lord's desire to heal and the power inherent in our wonderfully sacramental Church to bring this about. The reality that *healing* is one of the charismatic gifts given to the early churches and taught by Paul in First Corinthians, Chapter Twelve, to be bestowed by the Spirit, might explain why healing entered into our present day Catholic lifestyle through the *release of the Spirit*—that Charismatic Experience mentioned earlier in this discussion.

It would be a mistake of some magnitude if misunderstanding or distrust of the Charismatic Renewal Movement deprived the Catholic community of this amazing sign of our times, that Jesus is healing in every way, today.

A brief bibliography on the subject of healing in the Catholic context:

MacNutt, Francis, OP, *Healing* (Ave Maria Press: Notre Dame), 1974.

——, *The Power To Heal* (Ave Maria: Notre Dame), 1977.

Shlemon, Barbara, *Healing Prayer* (Ave Maria Press: Notre Dame), 1976.

Shlemon, Barbara and Linn, Matthew and Dennis, *To Heal As Jesus Heals* (Sacrament of Anointing of the Sick) (Ave Maria Press: Notre Dame), 1978.

Linn, Matthew and Dennis, *Healing of Memories* (Paulist Press: New Jersey), 1974.

——, *Healing Life's Hurts* (integration of forgiveness with Kubler-Ross stages) Paulist Press: New Jersey), 1977.

Scanlan, Michael, TOR, *Inner Healing* (Paulist Press: New York), 1974.

Sanford, Agnes, *The Healing Light* (Logos: Plainfield, New Jersey), 1947.

Basic Renewal of Parish Life

THE ultimate question about parish life and its reason for existence has yet to be asked. It might come out something like this:

Does the presence of St. Mary's have an impact upon the quality of life and love in *this* suburb?

Would it make a significant difference in *this* neighborhood if St. Mary's were forced to move to another area?

Would its departure be keenly felt as a loss to the civic community?

If we must answer "no" then what does this have to say for the ability of the parish to touch its environment with the Spirit of Jesus and the gospel vision that he offers? If church is not influencing society towards transformation into wholeness and justice, then why church, why *this* local parish?

All of the elements for a deepening of parish life seem to be contained in the basic Christian community that is conscious of Jesus as its head, nourished by his Word and Bread, and able to reach out under his power to transform sin into justice and sickness in all of its disguises into wholeness. When this is the experience of a local parish, Jesus lives in the city through his many brothers and sisters. That local church is known and cherished by all. How often does one actually encounter a genuine community powerful enough in witness and sufficiently united in strength to effect neighborhood renewal?

The gradual maturation of charismatic prayer groups into Christian communities is, at least, a conscious effort in this direction. Many lay men and women, as they discover charismatic gifts and gospel insight, become eager to serve more directly in their local parishes and to make the Lord more known in their neighborhoods. Revised sacramental rites and extension of new ministries to the lay church have opened up various possibilities and people are ready. Yet, pastors are often reticent to offer such roles to the members of their own parish prayer groups.

The position of the American bishops is clear on this point. A document prepared by the United States Bishops' Committee on Doctrine and presented to the entire Bishops' Conference in Chicago in May, 1979, makes the following statements:

> In defining "ministry" one must keep in mind that it is above all the response to the call to serve that Christ makes to the entire Church. As history shows, this service is always open to further exploration and understanding. . . .

> Above all, the Council affirmed the personal and corporate responsibility of all adult members for the life and mission of the Church. In practice, this means the need to explore fully and courageously the charisms and service of the laity, and to allow scope for their use and development.

Several comments from Bishop Raymond Lucker of the Diocese of New Ulm in Minnesota in a recent interview simplify the question even further:

> Development of the ministry concept must take place within communities of believing people who pray together, share, love one another, and who are open to the Spirit. . . . Our people don't yet understand that every single member of the church has the responsibility of ministry to others, to act as Jesus would have in relation to people in our own communities. (National Catholic Reporter, June 1, 1979)

Charismatic giftedness does open a parish to great vitality measured on the one hand by the willingness and generosity of church members, lay and ordained, to serve one another in the community and neighborhood in a loving, healing way, and, on the other hand by the readiness of the ordained to accept and free such giftedness for service in the Spirit.

Liturgical roles of lector, auxiliary minister of communion, leader of song; visitation of the sick with prayer for healing in hospital and home; teaching of Scripture and evangelization of adults and children; lay-ordained retreat teams—fresh opportunities continue to emerge for those who have eyes that want to see. Numerous charismatic communities have already integrated their style of life and spirituality into the local parish and everyone has been the better for it. Resourceful parish staffs are discovering that, with discernment and guidance, a veritable gold mine of sound apostolic lay people, grounded in Scripture and strengthened by frequent Eucharist, are at their disposal to minister wherever the needs of their parish send them. Where the charisms of a prayerful community are at work, there is life in the Spirit of Jesus.

Cardinal Leon-Josef Suenens has called this "a new Pentecost" that naturally followed from the rock-bottom renewal that the Second Vatican Council effected in the Church. Ought it to be so surprising that the Spirit would raise up so many ministries and ministering people, and that he should release new and strange charisms—strange because his Church had ceased to remember or expect the power of the Acts of the Apostles in this age?

Admittedly, this presentation might smack of unreality and, perhaps, a bit of emotional euphoria from behind rose-colored glasses. Community—yes, but why intense? Healing—well maybe. But quietly, please, and don't ask for a miracle! Justice—be realistic; today's problems are enormous. Let me be the first to admit that my hopes for the Charismatic Renewal don't always materialize and that my experiences with prayer groups and charismatic lifestyle have not always been good ones. We are learning! But, allow me also to conclude with an account of a family in genuine need and a charismatic prayer group that quietly but selflessly met that need. It is experiences such as this that bolster my hopes and encourage my endurance in a young movement that does, for all of its weaknesses, attempt to love radically.

It happened in Dolton, Illinois, that an elderly couple, new in the neighborhood, came upon hard times. The husband, in his late seventies, had been suffering from serious heart disease for years; then three years ago, debilitation began to set in and he could no longer drive. In this small suburb, there was no way to move unless one drove and suddenly this couple found themselves cut off from church, grocery shopping, everything.

Their oldest daughter lived a distance away, but heard that there was a charismatic group in the local parish, St. Jude the Apostle Church, and so she phoned the rectory asking for assistance from them. It happened that the young priest celebrated Eucharist for this group and so he spoke with her and reassured her that her parents would be taken care of.

From that day on, for three years, the couple was driven to church on Sunday without fail and their shopping needs were provided for. Everyone pitched in and it seemed a burden to no one. Four months ago, the husband began to fail so rapidly that it became necessary to seek rehabilitation for him. The family's pain over this decision was agonizing. To make things harder, it was Chicago's worst winter and seven feet of snow made roads nearly impassable. Even the couple's sons could not get to them.

Yet, somehow, the charismatic cars got through. In the midst of a sub-zero freeze, the husband died and even then, the charismatic community offered the strength of its presence and its concern. The widow lives on with the friendship and solicitous support of this beautiful group of people.

Who are they? Twenty or so upper middle-agers and young adults, some married couples among them, who gather on Thursday evenings to meet the Lord Jesus in his Word, his Bread, and one another.

What do they do besides pray? Their ministry in this large suburban parish is to reach out to those who are not helped by anyone else: the elderly and infirm shut-ins who live on the island of "isolation" in a large metropolitan society where people are expected to take care of themselves, and the abandoned in the local hospital and nursing home who are expected to live on to the end of their lives alone.

Why do I have great confidence in the strength and holiness of the Charismatic Renewal as it expresses itself through communities such as the St. Jude Prayer Group? Why have I given my time to sharing all of this with you? Perhaps, because that elderly couple are my father and mother. Perhaps, because I have truly met the Lord Jesus in the selfless love of charismatic community and want to pass it on.